HOUSES FOR THE 21ST CENTURY

PERIPLUS

Published in 2004 by Periplus Editions (HK) Ltd.,
by arrangement with Pesaro Publishing, Sydney, Australia.

Editor: Patrick Bingham-Hall 2000
Designer: Patrick Leong
All Photography: Copyright © Patrick Bingham-Hall
Text Copyright © Pesaro Publishing

ISBN 0-7946-0199-5

Distributed by:

North America, Latin America & Europe
Tuttle Publishing
Airport Industrial Park
364 Innovation Drive
North Clarendon, VT 05759-9436
Tel: (802) 773 8930 Fax: (802) 773 6993
Email: info@tuttlepublishing.com

Japan
Tuttle Publishing
Yaekari Building, 3rd Floor,
5-4-12 Osaki, Shinagawa-ku
Tokyo 141-0032
Tel: (03) 5437 0171 Fax: (03) 5437 0755
Email: tuttle-sales@gol.com

Asia Pacific
Berkeley Books Pte. Ltd.
130 Joo Seng Road, #06-01/03
Singapore 368357
Tel: (65) 6280 1330 Fax: (65) 6280 6290
Email: inquiries@periplus.com.sg

Colour Origination Universal Graphics, Singapore
Printed and Bound by Star Standard, Singapore
08 07 06 05 04   6 5 4 3 2 1

Front Cover Image: Harbour House
Newcastle, NSW, Australia 2003
Architect Stutchbury and Pape with Bourne Blue

N House Brisbane, Australia 2003 >
Architect: Donovan Hill

HOUSES
FOR THE
21ST CENTURY

Text Editor: Geoffrey London

General Editor: Patrick Bingham-Hall

Essays by Anoma Pieris Amanda Achmadi
Philip Goad Pirak Anurakyawachon
Geoffrey London Paul Walker & Justine Clark

Photography by Patrick Bingham-Hall

CONTENTS

Courtyard House Bali, Indonesia 2003
Architect: CY Kuan

Hua Guan House Singapore 1999–2001
Architect: WOHA Architects

THE 21ST CENTURY HOUSE

BY GEOFFREY LONDON

Geoffrey London is Professor of Architecture at the School of Architecture and Fine Arts, The University of Western Australia.

Of all architectural forms, houses are the most culturally sensitive to their times, so what could we expect to see in a '21st Century House'? What could distinguish these houses from those that preceded them?

An interest in the new, and especially in new forms of housing, was an ongoing preoccupation of 20th Century Western architecture. Histories of this period revolve around projections for the 'future house', often directed by utopian conviction in the potential for architects to reform peoples' lives. And the instrument for this reformation was to be technology and the possibilities that would ensue. From the days of the Bauhaus, when Walter Gropius and his fellow Bauhauslers proposed the industry-produced house 'Am Horn', the belief in what technology could deliver has been a powerful article of faith. Architectural form, and the design of interiors, accordingly developed in response to assumptions about technological change, often anticipating and projecting 'future house' types and forms.

After WWII this view erupted with optimism in the economic recovery, reflected in the eager embrace of American consumerism – specifically the new products for the home, developed through advances in technology.

With his iconic collage *Just What Is It That Makes Today's Homes So Different, So Appealing?*, Richard Hamilton revealed a sardonic vision of a new domestic world. The collage, an early example of what became known as Pop Art, formed the life-size poster placed at the entrance of the exhibition 'This is Tomorrow' held at London's Whitechapel Art Gallery in 1956. In it can be seen fragments taken from popular culture, the world of advertising and the promotion of consumerism. It was the brave new post-war world,

Richard Hamilton 'Just What Is It That Makes Today's Homes So Different, So Appealing?' Kunsthalle, Tubingen

looking forward to a new start, a future aided by the promises of technological invention. And the exhibition was in London, one of the acknowledged centres of cultural production, which was to be found, of course, in either Europe or the USA.

In the Daily Mail Ideal Homes Exhibition, also held in London in 1956, Alison and Peter Smithsons' 'House of the Future' was the architectural equivalent of Hamilton's collage. The House of the Future, projected to a future 1980, was to be a completely self-contained town house, making maximum possible use of new manufacturing techniques, new materials and the most advanced domestic appliances available. It was actually commissioned as a backdrop, a container for the latest domestic gadgets just out of prototype stage.[2] The house was to be capable of mass production in the same way as a motorcar and, like the motorcar, was to be a symbol of a technologically enlightened way of life, an item of consumption with built-in obsolescence. The Smithsons' aim was proletarian, it was to be a project that made available the latest advances for everyman, following on from the aspirations of the pre-war utopian architectural Modernists.

It assumed a densely populated urban setting and the nearby presence of the public world of the street to relieve the introversion of its private world. Its key formal characteristic was a continuous surface, intended originally to be constructed from the new material of reinforced plastic, but (because of time limitations) was built more conventionally of plywood. The moulded form was to contain storage, furniture, and services, and its seamless surfaces allowed an appreciation of the house as a whole piece, as a fully determined 'product' derived from the latest in technological advances.

The 'House of the Future' proved very popular with exhibition visitors, though Jacques Tati lampooned the same possibility in his 1958 film, *Mon Oncle*, in which his bumbling Luddite alter ego, Monsieur Hulot, is forced into absurd situations by technology running amok. The setting is a futuristic house where everything is controlled by push buttons and machines. In this film, Tati pursues the theme of addiction to technology and questions its motivation through a series of comical incidents of man versus machine.

Individuals like Richard Buckminster Fuller had no such doubts. He had been promoting the potential of technology to assist housing since the late 1920s with his light-weight 'Dymaxion' houses, based on construction principles from the new airplane industry, to be prefabricated and delivered to site by a dirigible. Fuller enjoyed great popularity in the 1960s, especially in Australia where he influenced a whole generation of architects. He was the major speaker at a 1966 student-organised conference in Perth, after which a rash of his trademark geodesic domes blossomed across the country.

The Archigram group in London followed on from the Smithsons in the 1960s and, with a comic-book approach to technology, predicted a vision of a future urbanism seen through the frame of mass culture. This resulted in memorable images of walking cities, plug-in cities and sin cities. The 1960s was also the time of space exploration and, surely, it was argued, architecture should be responsive to such developments.

However, many architects following this period believed that attempts to legitimise architecture, and to make decisions about architectural form via other disciplines like science and the social sciences, led to an erosion of the discipline. Explorations of pure form reasserted those characteristics specific to the discipline, but this pursuit of autonomy alienated many practitioners and potential clients. The false hope of architectural autonomy is still playing itself out in the formalist experiments to be found, essentially in Europe and the USA.

Following the collapse of communism, the rise of globalisation, and extended periods of conservatism in global politics, architects are now less sanguine than their early 20th Century counterparts about the potential of architecture to effect change in society. They are less determined to assert powerful aspirations and modes, and are more content to produce individuality through modes that adjust, fine-tune, swerve and nudge. They also recognise the plurality of architectural positions, the impossibility of the single truth and the single mode of enquiry. Deyan Sudjic, in his book *Home: The Twentieth Century House*, concludes with the observation:

> At the close of the 20th Century, domestic architecture has never been a more permissive and inclusive subject. It is no longer necessary to belong to one camp or another.[3]

Half a century on from the 'House of the Future', what are the architectural preoccupations that might identify a house as being of the 21st Century? How will it relate to the technological aspirations of the previous century, and what will it show of the emerging values of the new century?

These were questions that motivated this book – questions initially posed in Australia, long regarded as on the fringe, on the periphery of global cultural production, a place where culture was received and modified, but rarely spawned. The book was to take the form of a speculation, early in the 21st Century, on what was emerging in new architect-designed houses and on what these houses may inform us about their society and their culture. As the book evolved, however, it was broadened to give equal importance to houses from countries encircling Australia as an acknowledgement of Australia's location in a region very different from those of the architectural models usually drawn upon in Australia – Europe and the United States. A characteristic of the 21st Century and the spread of globalisation is a de-centring, so that no single national cultural hegemony can be justified. And the region of which Australia indisputably forms a part, South Asia, is emerging as one of the most dynamic and diverse economic and cultural regions of the new century.

As houses were revealed in the region, the book became larger in its ambition and the Australian focus diminished. This has resulted in a multi-faceted view of the 21st Century house, one that is more pluralistic in its assertions than it would have been. It is a richer, more complex view, one that is inflected by the distinctive qualities of each country.

The houses that appear in the book are from Sri Lanka, India, Malaysia, Singapore, Indonesia, Australia and New Zealand (all postcolonial countries), and from Thailand, which miraculously escaped colonisation.

The region is marked by a history of climate-responsive residential architecture, with the single detached villa as the most valued and most sought after model for housing. It is also marked by extreme disparities between wealth and poverty, and by the legacies of colonial occupation. The search for an independent cultural identity, and for an architecture that is emblematic of that identity, is a recurring characteristic of the region.

'Black and White' house Goodwood Hill, Singapore
Early 1920s

The architecture examined in this book is refreshing, fashioned as it is so directly by political, social and climatic pressures, together with powerful individual ideas, resulting in a wide range of formal responses.

The selection of the houses was based on what might be recognised as exemplars of an emerging range of approaches. Unlike the Smithsons' 'House of the Future', it is not now possible to claim such a powerful single instance of a broadly supported approach. The houses selected reveal new concepts and responses to their particular conditions: geographic, climatic, social, economic and cultural.

Philip Goad's essay, 'A Concise History of Future Houses–On the 'Other' Side of the World', identifies three broad approaches in the houses selected for the book:

> ...architects working on this other side of the world have tended to follow three paths in thinking about the future house: 1) the single house as a modernist project that continues to tackle–but critically–the New World city's specificity of climate and colonial planning; 2) the use of alternative labour technologies as a response to the immediate circumstances of practice and issues of local political economy; and 3) the complete retreat from the city, the house as 'low-tech', small, and 'anti-bungalow' and reformist rather than nostalgic in aesthetic.

This book offers an overview, but one that is by necessity limited and partial. It is not attempting to be comprehensive, but to expose tendencies and to suggest possibilities that may have resonance beyond the region.

That the Smithsons' 'House of the Future' was never tangibly realized on any kind of scale is a measure of the tenacity with which the concept of 'house' is understood as something apart from the disposable space-age world of innovative technology to which the Smithsons and many others aspired.

Issues of comfort, security, privacy, and a symbolism that evokes these qualities, have proven more enduring than the dream of salvation by technology. This is understood well by those who market housing, those who promote a view of the house as our largest single investment, the house as an asset and sale-able commodity. How have architects responded to this understanding?

It is a global reality that only a very small percentage of all housing is designed by architects. Architects design (in the main) for the affluent. This is certainly the case in Asia where it is only the affluent who can afford the luxury of a single detached villa. Outside this fragment of the market, much new housing can be characterised as retreating to architectural imagery of the past. The use of such past forms reinforces the illusion of a return to a time of safety, predictability, and uniformity, a simulation of an idealised past, which is now preferred in a world of widespread and ongoing terrorism.

This cautious conservative approach has been given impetus by New Urbanism, a movement originating in the USA that has been adopted internationally with great enthusiasm.[4] The best known examples are the towns of Seaside[5] (used as the setting for the make-believe world of Truman in Peter Weir's film, *The Truman Show*), and Celebration, both in Florida, USA. The houses in these towns, at first glance, look no different from the houses of comfortable pre-war small-town USA. While the principles of New Urbanism are admirable, directed towards the establishment of community and the creation of safe, useable public spaces, the built outcomes do not suggest anything about contemporary culture beyond a rejection of the present and a desire to simulate the past.

A key aspect of New Urbanism is the high level of control exercised over building designs, normally through the device of 'pattern books' that set out architectural codes. These codes draw on traditional housing forms, thus leading to the term 'Neo-traditionalism', often used as another way of describing New Urbanism.

Changed methods of construction, new modes of technology, and evolving social and cultural values have had little effect on the architectural forms of New Urbanism. It is logical to assume that a level of architectural determinism is operating–as if by reproducing the forms of the past, the social values of the past will be reproduced or, at least, a highly idealised version of those values.

A global characteristic of affluent cities with ever-spreading suburbs is the diminution of the public realm and the consequent development of the 'monster house' that contains just about everything. The facilities once found on urban streets have been retreating to the individual house. The 'monster house' now contains a kitchen that could service a restaurant, a liquor bar, a coffee maker, a pool table, a swimming pool, a home cinema, and a karaoke bar. This signals a retreat to the private and secure-able compound fearing what lies without–for many, the 'monster house' is a fully serviced refuge from the dangers of the public realm. There is now no need to go out and engage with the threats beyond the electrical security gate–chaotic, uncontrollable, fearsome, and brought into the home safely through television. It is the ultimate form of privatisation and, as cities become more and more geared towards meeting individual or private desires, what are the implications for urban spaces and the public realm? Inevitably, their impoverishment will continue.

Reacting to these endemic international trends, which present us with a startlingly homogeneous suburban world, this book concentrates on opportunities for alternative architectural futures. By placing houses in Australia and New Zealand alongside houses from South Asia and Southeast Asia, the book invites contemplation as to how the architectural challenges of one place might usefully inform and influence those of another.

Resistance to an architectural orthodoxy associated with previous colonial or repressive regimes is a recurring theme in the book's South Asian essays. Anoma Pieris in her essay, 'Beyond the Vernacular House', makes the point that 'Western aspirations are strained through local cultural filters' and that, with an embrace of modern urban habits, new house forms are based on Western space requirements but are 'adapted to South Asian cultural traditions and behaviours.'

Two related strategies are harnessed to enable the application of such filters and adaptations. One is the vernacular, the means by which the local inflects the universal modern and allows local identity to be established. The other is the use of climatic factors as a major determinant of architectural form.

Manel Nivasa House Colombo, Sri Lanka 2000–2003
Architect: Hiranti Welandawe

The response to the vernacular embraces not only questions of architectural form, but also local building conventions. In the case of Sri Lanka, the development of a modern vernacular had a political dimension with the prohibition of imported building materials leading to a reliance on local technique. However, the Sri Lankan architects selected for this book, the 'next generation', demonstrate what Pieris calls 'looking beyond vernacular architecture', with modern urban demands resulting in 'alternative expressions of everyday life for modern Sri Lankans.'

The use of modern Western forms in Indonesia is associated with Suharto's expedient construct of an imagined 'modern Indonesia' which was, in fact, a misrepresentation of the reality of life under his rule. The introduction of vernacular elements is seen by Amanda Achmadi in her essay as a

Ciganjur House Jakarta, Indonesia 2003
Architect: Adi Purnomo

conscious subversion of this distortion, albeit by a small number of architects. She describes the process of reinterpretation of the traditional methods of dealing with the specifics of that place as a means of re-establishing Indonesian identity. Deployment of aspects of the vernacular becomes the means whereby the architectural profession may address its bad conscience arising from its contribution to presenting 'the fiction of modern Indonesia' – the modern housing estates that displaced and further marginalised the traditional kampongs. Achmadi describes the most recent

architectural experiments that have as their major aspiration the enabling of a local way of life, rather than providing a public demonstration of claimed status.

She also introduces a project of a more modest nature in the form of temporary housing for low-income workers in Jakarta, who would otherwise be required to commute great distances. This, it's suggested, points the way for a more substantial engagement by architects with the under-privileged majority of the population.

There is a direct relationship between vernacular technique and building forms derived from responses to climatic conditions. Engagement with such strategies for cooling and for building provides a means of asserting local differences, of rejecting architectural universalism. And yet, climate responsive architecture also carries a legacy of colonial assumptions, of a certain way of life made possible by exploitation.

Pirak Anurakyawachon, in his discussion of recent Thai houses, writes of the influence of the West and the fusion of Western Modernist forms with Eastern cultural structures. From this he seeks a response to the reality of life in Thailand, rather than the production of architectural imagery that represents an assumed way of life or a compulsion to be Westernised.

The migration of influence is not one way. For example, Australian domestic architecture has undoubtedly been receptive to Asian ways of living, encouraged by the large numbers of Asians moving to live in Australia, and by the large numbers of Australians visiting and living in the surrounding Asian countries. Philip Goad describes '...that eternally captivating search in Australian architecture, the semi-enclosed outdoor space – the ideal place in which to dwell in this country...'. This search has been made more productive as a result of studying and understanding Asian ways of living. And some of Australia's best architects have chosen to live and work in Asia. For example, Kerry Hill has spent over thirty years working in Asia and being receptive to the traditions of the East has significantly enriched his crisp Modernist work. And he, in turn, has been an important mentor for many young Asian architects.

The pursuit of cultural identity and the establishment of 'geographic belonging' through domestic architecture is another recurring theme in the book, supported by the same twin strategies of the vernacular and climate. This, however, has its problems, as outlined by Pieris in her essay on the tropical house in Malaysia and Singapore. She introduces the concept of 'neo-tropicality' – a commodification of the tropical, the pursuit of picturesque imagery and, a kind of South Asian New Urbanism. The houses selected for the book from these countries resist this easy conformity.

Another theme is the rise of an affluent middle class, a new client base for the local architects. Achmadi entitles her essay 'Indonesia: The Emergence of a New Architectural Consciousness of the Urban Middle Classes.' Affluence and aspirations to affluence may very well be the dominant reality, especially in previously impoverished, low-tech 'Third World' countries in Asia. In this regard, it's useful to record the observation by Thomas Friedman in his book, *The Lexus and The Olive Tree:*

> ...what many of these (Indonesian) educated twenty- and thirty-year-olds had in common was that they wanted to get rich, without having to be corrupt, and they wanted democracy, but they didn't want to go in the streets and fight for it...their whole strategy was to do everything they could...to integrate Indonesia into the global system. They hoped that by tying Indonesia into these global institutions and markets – whether it was to the World Trade Organization, Pizza Hut, APEC, ASEAN, Merrill Lynch...they might be able to import from beyond the standards and rules-based systems that they knew would never be initiated from above and could never be generated from below.

Auroville, an international community in South India, is discussed in the essay by Anoma Pieris, 'Beyond the Vernacular House'. It offers a small case study taken from an architectural group that has rigorously approached the question of sustainability in their housing, and made considered use of local building practices and climatic strategies. Auroville is a utopian community, a mix of East and West, of modern and vernacular, a real condenser of many of the issues raised in the essays.

In Australia and New Zealand, there is the ongoing issue of landscape and its relation to houses, further evidence of the uncertainty of how to occupy these 'strange' countries. Philip Goad notes that the Australian houses deal '...with a landscape – neither in fear or loathing of it, nor in its triumphant conquest – but by celebrating its individuality...'. Justine Clark and Paul Walker, in their essay on New Zealand houses, articulate the ongoing relationship to landscape, observing that local architecture '...is deeply affected by the preoccupation with landscape.' They identify the house embedded in the landscape, the house as landscape, and the house as a form of negotiation with the landscape. In contrast they note that New Zealand architecture is only '...beginning to come to terms with the country's non-Western heritage.' They also suggest that there is an urgent need for a '... rethinking of the house with the emergent multi-culturalism of NZ cities.'

Goad recognises a shift in the location of the Australian houses selected for the book, with seven of these ten houses in inner city suburbs, dealing with urban issues 'rarely associated by international readers with the stereotypical images of Australian domestic architecture...'. As Australian cities attempt to consolidate and address urban sprawl, architects are now locked into '...accompanying labyrinthine planning controls and belligerently defended heritage overlays...' imposed by local authorities. This has led to housing experiments quite different from those of fifty years earlier when architects, more typically, were working on new subdivision sites.

When compared with the Smithsons' 'House of the Future', houses for the 21st Century are no longer bewitched by the utopian possibilities of advanced technology. Any universal utopianism seems unlikely in these more knowing, less optimistic times – the houses demonstrate a response to what is known and tangible. There is a strong interest in the tactile – the quality, texture and presence of materiality rather than immateriality. There is a preference for substance, rather than the absence that characterised so much late 20th Century minimalist architecture. The materials are local, with several instances of inventive recycling. Many of the houses offer carefully considered critiques of what has preceded them, in political, cultural and architectural terms. They are deeply connected with their sites and with their location, and respond directly to local climate and to social conventions. They are not abstract objects that could be found in any other city in the world. In the face of growing globalisation, it is to their specificity that they lay claim.

NOTES

1 A. & P. Smithson, 'House of the Future at the Ideal Homes Exhibition', *Architectural Design*, March 1956, pp.101-102.

2 For a full discussion on the House of the Future see Irenee Scalbert, 'Towards a Formless Architecture: The House of the Future by A+P Smithson', *Archis*, 1999, September, no.9, p.34–47.

3 Deyan Sudjic with Tulga Beyerle, *Home: The Twentieth Century House*, London: Lawrence King Publishing, 1999, p.103.

4 Peter Katz, *The New Urbanism: Towards an Architecture of Community*, New York, McGraw Hill, 1994,

5 See David Mohney and Keller Easterling (editors), *Seaside: Making a Town in America*, New York: Princeton Architectural Press, 1991, and Todd Bressi (editor), *The Seaside Debates: a critique of the new urbanism*, New York: Rizzoli, 2002.

6 For a fuller development of this argument against New Urbanism, see Geoffrey London, 'In Celebration', in *TAKE 1: Urban Solutions, Propositions for the future Australian city*, edited by McGauran, Robert, Canberra: Royal Australian Institute of Architects, 2002.

7 Thomas Friedman, *The Lexus and The Olive Tree*, London: Harper Collins,1999, p.143.

Waitamariki House Northland, New Zealand 1998 >
Architect: Mitchell and Stout

OUTSIDE THE TROPICAL HOUSE

BY ANOMA PIERIS

Anoma Pieris has degrees from the University of Moratuwa, Sri Lanka and the Massachusetts Institute of Technology. She has practiced as an architect in Sri Lanka and in Singapore.

The 'Tropical House' suggests a built environment in harmony with a very particular climate. During the past decade it has been the focus of many Southeast Asian journals and publications, mostly originating in Singapore.[1] Yet discussions of the 'Tropical House' in Singapore describe the yearning for landed property in a context where the house, the home and domesticity itself, are couched in very different terms. Landed housing is as rare in Singapore as it may be in Hong Kong, Bombay or New York and is priced accordingly. The 'house', in a land-scarce city-state, is a utopian ideal against which other alternatives are frequently imagined. In Singapore, the bungalow, which we associate with post-colonial contexts, is more often the privilege of a few wealthy Singaporeans and Western expatriates.

A Singaporean 'Neo-Tropicality', as the trend was labelled (by professionals and academics alike), is a curious hybrid of vernacular experiences and 1970s Modernism.[2] In the Asian 'Tropical House', the homeowner sits in the air-conditioned comfort of the interior space and looks out at a scenographic view of the natural environment. Vast areas of glazing protect the viewer from the scorching heat and monsoon rain, and the bugs, snakes, mosquitoes and geckos that might destroy the romance of an idealised tropical experience. For a population that is distributed in a monolithic landscape of apartment block towers (designed frugally as a 1970s social experiment), the romanticising of landed housing is seen in affiliation with the regional culture of tourism. Equally, the government monopoly on public housing leaves local architects with a very small margin for experimentation. The 'Tropical House', which has been researched extensively and promoted by writers such as Robert Powell, Tan Hock Beng and William Lim, is

Eu House Singapore 1994
Architect: Ernesto Bedmar

consequently confined to Singapore's top layer of elite residences.[3]

To understand the yearning for the 'Tropical House' it is necessary to delve deeply into a fifty-year old history of climatically-determined architecture and to scrutinise its origins. It is important to note that independence for Singapore and Malaysia came relatively late, at the end of

1950s, after hard-core nationalism in South Asia (India and Sri Lanka) had exhausted its quota of blood, sweat and tears. While an unusual marriage of genius loci with the picturesque tradition was evolving across the Bay of Bengal, Southeast Asian nationalism eagerly embraced Modernism . The 'vernacular' remained a very separate discourse, related to pre-modern communities in rural environments. The desire to construct a sense of 'geographic belonging' in a culturally-diverse migrant context that had been educated, and imagined (as in the case of Singapore) through colonial architecture, provoked serious attention to climate. In the context of Singapore and Malaysia, 'tropicality' played a new role in providing a neutral template, diffusing ethnocentric or essentialist divisions. However, although 'climate' was a place-specific attribute, it inherited many colonial assumptions that were associated with tropical life and were interpreted through orientalist attitudes. In the post-colonial context 'tropical' architecture had the additional task of proving its modernity against such associations. In combination, both the neutral template and the historic discourse paved the way for a new discursive estrangement of an everyday reality, providing a romantic respite from the hectic pace of urban development.

As Singapore catapulted into First World status, the Singapore house stepped back into that frozen time capsule of tropical life that, with rising real estate prices, had been transformed into an invaluable commodity for modern Singaporeans. 'Tropicality' was commodified, and directly serviced an explosion in regional resort tourism. The estrangement of the 'tropical' was further enabled by the migrant pasts of architects whose ancestors had come to Singapore from diverse climatic and cultural experiences. In the academic world, a 'tropical' discourse linked Southeast Asia to other equatorial contexts including South America and Africa. As the trend became publicised in Singapore, tropical features such as screens, sun shades and awnings began to appear almost randomly on various building surfaces with scant regard for the logic of the natural elements concerned.

There is, of course, much to be said for a truly climate sensitive architecture. The Singapore Conference Hall by

the Malayan Architects Co-Partnership, which was inaugurated in 1965, can be considered as one of the finest examples of this direction.[4] Despite local climatic devices such as ventilation panels, different methods of sun screening, and extended eaves, the Conference Hall remains, like Singapore, unapologetically Modern. The orientation of this early generation of 'Malayan' architects was channelled in diverse ways into the architecture of Tay Keng Soon, Ken Yeang, and William Lim, who have been widely published and have international reputations.[5] Ideas of environmental sustainability and climatically sensitive design were approached via a Modernist palette. The stylistic construction of the 'tropical', which followed during the late 1980s and the 1990s, came with a shift from this approach, with greater interest in the vernacular associations and the aesthetic implications of the 'tropical' for the burgeoning culture of Southeast Asian tourism. The next generation of architects revisited the picturesque possibilities of 'place' as a context for experiments with a particular brand of tropical Modernism in residential and resort architecture.

The challenge that faced the proponents of the 'tropical style' was the need to reconcile the modernity of Singaporean life with tactile domesticity and vernacular experiences. The clean lines and Cartesian forms with which they delineated the house from its tropical backdrop accentuated the suddenness with which modern citizens had been extracted from their *kampong* habitat and extruded into a grid of public apartments. Unlike the textured and tactile softness of the new and the traditional 'vernacular', Singapore's new 'Tropical House' was characterised by its very estrangement from the land and the climate. Its location against the landscape was pure geometric form, with a pristine interior often borrowed from minimalist trends in Japanese architecture. Construction was of a heavier aesthetic of concrete frame and masonry with tiled roof and plastered walls, and had not yet embraced industrial construction methods. Such labour-intensive construction soon became affordable, due to the deployment of inexpensive foreign labourers from elsewhere in the Asian region. Although political, in its initial opposition to the unbridled dissemination of the International Style through State sponsored architecture, underlying the tropical agenda was the tacit understanding that a climatic ideology could be safely developed in Singapore and Southeast Asia without disrupting or disturbing the ideologies of governance.

REDEFINING THE HOUSE

The spacious two-storey detached residences that are featured in most books on Asian architecture exemplify the 'good class' bungalow, the most exclusive of Singapore's dwelling spaces. Since the majority of Singaporeans have no access to such environments, they provide us with little understanding of the meaning of 'house' for regional residents. 'Tropical' as defined through elite architectural projects is an inadequate category for the representation of the social hierarchies and political tensions that underwrite Asia's accelerated economic transformations.

Southeast Asia is unique for its 'tiger' economies, which are directed at creating an urban middle-class population. Singaporeans, although technologically savvy and cosmopolitan in orientation, have traded political freedoms for economic advancement. The aspirations of this new polity, although embodied in home ownership, are not reflected by Western style suburban growth. The pressure to raise the basic standard of living for large population groups

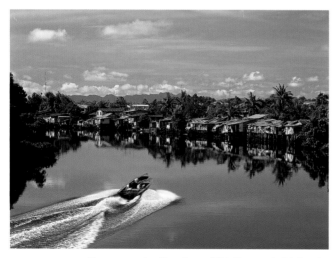

Kampong by the river Miri, Sarawak, Malaysia

is met through urban apartments or compact terrace housing projects, rather than the traditional spread of suburbs. In Malaysia, the developer-driven compaction of suburban growth occurs in isolated pockets, in areas far outside the commercial centres. In Singapore, public housing and mortgage payments underwrite citizenship loyalties and define middle-class home ownership through a high-rise apartment culture. Ideas of 'house', 'place' and 'climate' in both these contexts are affected by such experiences.

For this reason a review of the house in Singapore and Malaysia for the 21st Century needs to step outside the 'Tropical' frame and seriously regard, the implications of living in that region. The house as we know it has to be re-interpreted in all its local permutations including a *kampong* (village) house, a shophouse, a terrace house, an apartment and a condominium. A study of Southeast Asian architecture has yet to discuss the relevance of architectural solutions for the aspirations of an increasingly middle-class polity. Our search for the 21st Century Southeast Asian house is challenging for exactly these reasons.

VERNACULAR EXAMPLES

The major difference between the vernacular revival in South Asia and Southeast Asia can be traced to the economic difference between the two regions. In Sri Lanka and India, the return to vernacular methods was a product of an introverted economic policy and consequent self-reliance. In Singapore and Malaysia, free markets and increasing prosperity affected the perception of the vernacular, and the pre-history of the house was identified through a double lineage, rural and urban. The rural past was associated with pre-modern *kampongs* (villages), which shaped 'Malay' houses, while the urban past was represented using Chinese shophouses. These two types in turn provoked separate legacies of bungalows and terrace houses.

The *kampong* house, usually associated with Malay life, is a unique solution to the damp and marshy terrain of Southeast Asia and is typically elevated on stilts. Built in timber and *attap* (woven palm fronds) it is a pragmatic solution to the constant ventilation craved in the tropical heat and to the levels of safety necessary for rural dwelling. The area beneath the house acts as a social gathering space, a storage space and a barn. Aromatic fires lit beneath the elevated floor of the house are used to fumigate the house against mosquitoes during the evening. In the most elegant examples of these houses, the entire panelling is woven and replenished, demonstrating the constant attention paid by rural folk to the care of their dwelling spaces. While each house is inhabited by an extended family, the houses in each village are organised in reciprocal clusters projecting the spirit of community that binds village life.

During the British Colonial period in Singapore (1819–1959) and Malaysia (1795–1957), the idea of the elevated house, and the climatic advantages offered, inspired the raised bungalow constructed on masonry arches or stud columns. Although the space beneath often became a cellar for junk, it was a very different approach to the heavy plinth foundations of South Asian Colonial architecture. Many of the colonial residences built at the beginning of the 20th Century chose to adopt this approach as a solution to the damp and the humidity of a tropical climate. For example, Government House in Singapore (the official residence of the Prime Minister) is raised five feet above the ground for this purpose. More recent examples of architectural projects that adopt this model include: Jimmy Lim's Lim House – where he experiments with the tectonic of timber construction, and William Lim's Reuter House – where the organization is of pavilion style spaces. Jimmy Lim's Salinger House and Kerry Hill's Datai Hotel in Langkawi embrace stilt architecture. In each of these projects climatic responses borrow creatively from vernacular solutions.

The major problems faced by architects who transfer the qualities of a Malay House to a contemporary architectural project lie in the tendency to essentialise the Malays, or romanticise rural poverty as an idealized pre-modern mode of existence. Class and cultural boundaries between the urban elites and the rural or tribal sources of vernacular architecture often convert its appropriation into a predatory act with colonial underpinnings. Ideas of timelessness, cultural tourism and nationalist rhetoric equally exploit these architectures, converting them into artefacts that contrast

Shophouses Tanjong Pagar, Singapore

sharply with Asia's modern aspirations. The transformation from a communal to an individualistic life-style is achieved more readily in the urban housing types that absorbed colonial influences.

The urban house type that arrived in Singapore with Chinese migration was the shophouse, a combination of residential and commercial space provoked by colonial regulation and taxation. The interior of the shophouse was a tube-like introverted space between party walls, which established the width of all the interior spaces. The need to accommodate outdoor customs within this indoor arrangement created multiple courtyards organised in degrees from most public to private. In her book 'Contesting Space', Brenda Yeoh observes that the occupation of the shophouse was difficult to codify because of its division into semi-private compartments for an extended family system.[6] Moreover the appropriation of the public walkways as private verandah space conflated the public and the private divisions, making the shophouse 'illegible' in comparison with its European equivalents. The shophouse provided a neutral envelope that accommodated numerous activities, expanding the window of economic opportunity for native traders. Brothels, opium dens, gambling houses and secret societies were as much at home in the native landscape of the shophouses as the commercial and residential spaces. Perhaps for these very reasons, this became the primary site of urban gentrification during the 1990s, and the target of a new policy of conservation for adaptive re-use.

A number of architects in Singapore have undertaken shophouse renovation projects. These projects are unusual in their reconceptualisation of the interior space by the treatment of courtyard spaces and the manipulation of light. Renovating the narrow spaces of the shophouse demands a more precise understanding of the light and humidity of a tropical climate than does bungalow architecture. Consequently in shophouse conservation projects the treatment of the section becomes its dominant design feature. Many of Singapore's architects, including SCDA, Kerry Hill, Bedmar and Shi, WOHA and Richard Ho occupy or have occupied shophouses which have been converted for commercial purposes. These buildings provide some of the most interesting examples of architectural strategies for the adaptive re-use of residential environments. However, the rapid gentrification of shophouses for commerce steals away the 'life' of a residential neighbourhood and comes with attendant problems. As the shop takes over the house in this mixed typology, its meaning as a dwelling is relegated to the inadequate memories evoked by its conservation.

New terrace housing Miri, Sarawak, Malaysia

The closest urban derivative of the shophouse is the terrace house, a ubiquitous presence in Malaysia's new suburbs. The monotonous repetition of the same module throughout freshly created acreage is reminiscent of American sprawl. Unlike their shophouse antecedents, these houses are not mixed-use projects and are more closely related to European zoning patterns. In Malaysia, where land scarcity is not an the issue it is in Singapore, urbanisation occurs at its own pace, and cultural associations take precedence over climate. The terrace house has evolved into the semi-detached house more typically found in Singapore's early suburbs. Here a shared party wall separates two buildings that mirror one another. The 'Khoo House' designed by Ken Lou, and 'Resident Eight' designed by Ernesto Bedmar, apply a Modernist vocabulary to this type while utilizing the device of the shared light of shophouse architecture. The next step up in housing types would be the 'good class bungalow' which would be designed in a Modern tropical style, adding to the epidemic of an eclectic collage of architectural styles from Europe and Asia - popularly known as 'monster houses'.

INSIDE THE 'TROPICAL HOUSE'

The spatial divisions inside the houses in Singapore and Malaysia are not dissimilar. While a shrine room, prayer room or karaoke room may suggest the cultural preferences of the inhabitants, what roots them in their geographic locations are the service areas, which cater for the particularities of each ethnic group's diet. In the bungalow there will be an outdoor cooking space for the grinding, pounding and cleaning of raw ingredients. Grinding stones, pestle and mortar, wok burner and industrial sink all service the sophisticated demands of the Asian palate, and there will be a small ill-ventilated half-room tucked away in a corner with a squatting toilet, for the inevitable foreign maid from the Philippines, Indonesia or Sri Lanka. Even private apartments, such as those in condominium complexes anticipate these particular needs.

The major living spaces do not alter much from Western models. Air conditioning is ubiquitous. In good class bungalows the entertainment areas are furnished in plush and forbidding upholstery, leaving the family room for relaxation. The ascendance of the family room, which often doubles up as a play room, and houses the home entertainment and karaoke system, suggests the continued importance of the family activities in a modern environment. The Singaporean and Malaysian family, whether living in public housing apartments or landed housing, typically spans three generations.

The division between the wealthy and the middle-class Singaporean hardens at the boundary of the dwelling unit, where private garden space is the privilege of a select few. The colonial legacy lives on with a lawn, flowering shrubs and carefully placed ornamental tropical plants. The pool is increasingly a part of the Singapore house, despite the importation of much of its water. Natural surfaces are typically paved, bringing the cleanliness of the street up the driveway through the yard and into the tiled interiors. The clear boundary between exterior and interior climate ensures that the house is preserved as a distinct and introverted space, despite its views into the adjacent tropical environment.

Many Singapore and Malaysian architects have experimented with regional influences in bungalow architecture. They use pools, selective planting, contrasting textures and the play of light and dark to self-consciously construct the tropical context for their architecture. Collectively, their efforts have redefined an exclusive life-style adapted for the tropics through architecture. William Lim, Ernesto Bedmar, Kerry Hill, SCDA and CSYA are among those who have explored this approach in residential and resort architecture. However, their experiments remain at the level of formal considerations and have yet to re-examine those programmatic or social agendas, which first inspired European Modernist interventions.

APARTMENT DWELLERS

Despite the many published examples of landed housing types, there is no doubt that the true spirit of Singapore resides in its apartment complexes. The public housing neighbourhoods are widely described as 'the heartland' and are supported by up-to-date infrastructure and facilities in a

HDB Apartments Tampines New Town, Singapore

sustained effort at decentralisation. In the housing complex, as in the *kampong* or the shophouse street, family life spills out into the walkway and the void deck and wanders down into the hawker centres at the hub of each neighbourhood development. In Singapore and Malaysia, as in most of Southeast Asia, families come out into public spaces in the evening to eat, exercise or play sport. The restricted spaces of their apartment dwellings encourage such public interaction. In private condominiums, public areas and facilities within the complex limit such interaction to wealthy locals and expatriates. The monotony of the public housing project or the condominium block is broken by exaggerated attention to interior decoration. While the apartment blocks themselves provide a Modernist envelope, the apartments themselves are Post-Modern in their enthusiastic eclecticism. Every style of interior from traditional Chinese, Indian or Islamic, to

Coronation Road West House Singapore 1998
Architect: SCDA

Italianate, French, Pop or Balinese has had its moments.

While apartment living is equally available to all classes of Singapore society, in Malaysia it has very different connotations. Condominiums signal economic affluence and are coveted, despite the availability and affordability of landed properties. In comparison, the house in Malaysia is very much a detached building in a natural setting. Since palm oil and rubber are among the plantation industries in Malaysia and farming is very much a part of village life, the house cannot be separated from these associations which set the populations of the two nations apart, suggesting that they may have very different responses to a tropical climate. In this context, Singapore has lost an agrarian sensibility which can give other lives and meanings to the natural landscape, establishing the connections with climatic values intrinsic to everyday existence. Seasonal produce, market gardening, farm animals, herbs and other ingredients which may be relegated to the periphery of First World city life have, in Singapore, moved outside the national boundaries. The house, whatever its configuration, is ultimately an urban apartment. Re-conceptualizing Singapore's increasing urbanity while asserting its geographic setting has been the primary challenge for recent architects and for those in the next generation. Singapore has been produced through an

alienation from its tropical roots, and paradoxically, this inspires a rigorous pursuit of the tropical ideal.

Our search in the next generation of architects is for those courageous enough to break the mould and explore new ways of organising space, constructing habitual relationships or engaging textures. While their attention to detail and tectonic sensibilities must necessarily build on previous approaches, they need to challenge the inherent dependence on composition, which haunts the picturesque approach. It is through the refusal to define architecture within such frames that the most promising platforms for innovation can be constructed. What is urgently needed is an understanding of the flexibility of architectural ideas and a willingness to risk ignoring Western precedents. The first tentative steps in this direction suggest a movement away from picturesque imagery towards conceptual and tectonic considerations.

NOTES

1 Tan Hock Beng, *Tropical architecture and interiors : tradition-based design of Indonesia, Malaysia, Singapore, Thailand* /Page One publishers, 1994; *Tropical Retreats: The Poetics of place*/ Page One publishers 1996; *Tropical Paradise*/NY:HBI 2000.

Robert Powell, *The Tropical Asian House*/Select Books, 1996; *The Urban Asian House:Living in Tropical Cities*/Select Books,1998; *The New Asian House*/ Select publishers, 2001; *The Asian House : Contemporary Houses of Southeast Asia*/Select Books,1993.

Jane Doughty Marsden, New Asian Style: contemporary tropical living in Singapore/2002.

2 Low Boon Liang, Year 2001 - Neo-Tropicality, The Tropical Workshop Series, at the Department of Architecture, School of Design & Environment, NUS, Singapore Architect, 210/01, p174.

3 See endnote 1

4 The partnership included, Lim Chong Keat, William Lim Siew Wai, and Chen Voon Fee.

5 Robert Powell was author of: *Ken Yeang: rethinking the environment filter*, Landmark Books, 1989; *Rethinking the skyscraper: the complete architecture of Ken Yeang*, New York, Whitney Library of Design, 1999; *Line edge and shade: the search for a design language in tropical Asia: Tay Kheng Soon and Akitek Tenggara*, 1997.

6 Brenda Yeoh, Oxford University Press, 1996, p143–146.

Steel House, Jakarta, Indonesia 2002
Architect: Ahmad Djuhara

INDONESIA: THE EMERGENCE OF A NEW ARCHITECTURAL CONSCIOUSNESS OF THE URBAN MIDDLE CLASSES

BY AMANDA ACHMADI

Amanda Achmadi graduated as Bachelor of Architecture from Parahyangan University, Bandung, Indonesia. Amanda has worked as a practising architect in Jakarta and Bali.

ARCHITECTURAL IMAGINING OF 'MODERN' INDONESIA

To arrive at Jakarta International Airport and to drive into the centre of the city, is to be immediately confronted by the jungle of architectural paradox that is modern Indonesia. Side by side are contrasting architectural sequences. Patches of squatter settlements – perched on the banks of pitch-black rivers or chaotically cramped within irregularly shaped city blocks – stand in front, behind, or intertwined with complexes of towering high rise apartments and exclusive residential enclaves. The elevated highways of Jakarta provide a bird's eye view of the architectural and urban legacy of the rule of Suharto, the second President of Indonesia (1966–1998). The fragile urban pattern is composed of the architectural excesses of the 'upper' class and the architectural desperation of the urban poor. While Jakarta does not completely represent the urban complexity of Indonesia, the city's architectural contrasts have become the main model for the rest of the country. This is particularly so in housing, and it is not difficult to foresee a crisis to which this imbalance is heading.

The striking segregation between the 'modern' elements of the city and the *kampung* (the indigenous and informally laid out village settlements), is the most persisting phenomenon of the city's long-standing history, despite its major physical and political transformation. As Batavia, it was the main trading post of VOC/East Indies Trading Company (1619–1908) and subsequently the capital city of Dutch East Indies (1908–1942). As Jakarta it has been the capital city of Indonesia since 1945, and the base for successions of political power, where the ruling regime envisions and

View from elevated expressway Jakarta 2003

realises the imagined identity of the nation while, alongside, it appropriates and marginalises the indigenous *kampung*.[2] Between 1918 and 1921, during the Dutch colonial period, the residential complexes of Nieuw Gondangdia and Menteng were planned for the city's upper class which consisted of the Dutch community, European traders and influential natives. The complexes were designed by Ir. F.J. Kubatz and P.A.J Moojen, prominent members of the Municipal Department of Land and Housing in Batavia, and modelled on garden city ideas.[3] The architecture of the villa-type house units meticulously adapted Dutch art deco style into the tropical climate, a movement known as 'Dutch-Indies' architecture.[4] The complexes were built on unoccupied lands and plantation fields once cultivated by the surrounding *kampungs*. Between 1948 and 1953, the early years of Indonesia, a new satellite city called Kebayoran Baru was planned by architect and planner M. Soesilo of Central Planologisch Bureau.[5] It was designed for the public servants of the new government, and to ease the burden of the old city centre following the rapid growth of the city's post-war population. Built on a plantation field 8kms south of Menteng, the complex was strongly inspired by the Nieuw Gondangdia and Menteng. In both residential developments, neither social nor physical connections between the new city and the *kampung* were formally established. The *kampung* have never been considered as an element of the emerging society, as part of the planning of the colony, nor of the subsequent nation. While small-scale *kampung* improvement projects were initiated in both colonial and post-colonial periods[6], the efforts do not change the marginalisation of *kampung* within the broader housing and urban planning scheme. This worsened during the period of Suharto's New Order, where many kampungs were harshly replaced by 'modern' elements of the city.

In his study,[7] Abidin Kusno demonstrates that the production of housing architecture in Indonesia in the last three decades has been strongly shaped by the emergence of 'modern Indonesia,' an "imagined community" prescribed by Suharto's New Order regime.[8] This 'modern Indonesia' is introduced as an ordered society to replace Sukarno's concept of 'nation building', the former 'imagined

Jakarta kampung 2003

Indonesia', since projected by the New Order as the chaotic 'Old Order' Indonesia. The formulation of the 'modern Indonesia' promotes progress according to perceived International standards but, more importantly, also constrains Indonesian modern society within an economic and non-political realm in the name of socio-political 'stability'. Modern Indonesia is projected as a society capable of adopting the lifestyle of the developed First World[9] and social control is achieved by means of cultural propaganda. Ariel Heryanto argues that the New Order regime systematically authorized modes of interpretation through which culture is read and represented, not as a dynamic mechanism of cultivating life, but as a set of 'sacred' objects and objective realities detached from contemporary consciousness.[10] Culture is treated as a precious heritage that needs to be safeguarded by the contemporary generation. The result is not only an objectified culture, but also a society detached from the ideological mechanisms of cultural production. Such 'culture' loses its relevance in a 'modern' Indonesia that is so substantially defined by economic status.

The urban society of Indonesia has come to identify itself according to two contrasting categories of economic status: the 'upper-middle' class and the 'under' class.[11] Almost 60% of the urban population, mostly those of the 'under class', live in the kampung which are increasingly displaced and marginalized by the rapid growth of exclusive 'modern' housing of the minority 'upper-middle' class. This 'upper-middle' class is in fact comprised of two layers of society differentiated by their financial capacities. However, they share an identical dream of becoming and being a 'modern' Indonesia. Middle class societies (including those emerging from the 'under class'), along with their architecture remain invisible. The architectural paradox of Jakarta vividly suggests an absence of architectural production which would be created by middle class awareness of progressive cultural and economic practices, and critical and intellectual engagements with the wider urban social structure.[12]

The housing of 'modern Indonesia' has become an arena concerned with image making through which a certain desired identity can be claimed, despite the occupant's actual socio-economical status and mode of inhabitation. The privatisation of housing development in Indonesia since the late 1970s has fuelled this image making obsession, which prioritises the creation of a certain 'look' above other concerns. Dominant multinational property developers produce elite housing areas, curiously marked by First World images and architectural styles: Mediterranean, Japanese, Beverly Hills, and Spanish.[13] These images, widely circulated by television shows and the Hollywood movie industry, are profoundly perceived as signs of modernity *(moderen)* and progress *(kemajuan)*. These Western styled housing estates are built beside, or often in place of the increasingly underprivileged, architecturally and socially marginalized, *kampung.*[14]

WHEN THE DREAM IS SHATTERED: THE EMERGENCE OF THE MIDDLE CLASSES AND NEW ARCHITECTURAL EXPERIMENTATION

In 1998, after 3 decades, Suharto's regime came to a dramatic end. The year was marked by economic collapse, emergence of middle class political awareness through movements of students and public intellectuals, and violent riots in urban centres. The country was awoken from a dream by this devastating socio-cultural crisis. 'Upper middle' class Jakarta, whose architecture played a key role

in cementing the imagined and sharply divided 'modern Indonesia', was deliberately targeted during the riots alongside attacks on the ever discriminated against Indonesian-Chinese ethnic group.[15] Attacks on elite housing enclaves and the general reflection on Indonesia's social structure have led the profession of architecture to question its role in the making of 'modern Indonesia'. From this re-examination, it is hoped that new architectural propositions will emerge to challenge the perception of architecture as an image-making mechanism, an instrument which has significantly worsened the polarization of Indonesian modern society.

Five years on, housing experiments have started to emerge which propose the built environment as a place to live in and cultivate, rather than as the means to claim preferred status. The urban middle class and the architectural profession are developing a new architectural consciousness. Architectural practice is becoming shaped as a process addressing the need for a functioning and affordable built environment able to assist in the task of mending the polarized society. Beyond the burden of generating architectural styles, recent house projects demonstrate the way form-making engages with the creation of optimum spatial arrangement, wherein a decent life can be cultivated at any level of economic achievement.

RETHINKING THE MODE OF HABITATION, REFORMULATING HOUSE FORM

One aspect neglected in the design of elite housing estates is the functional and spatial programming of a house. Regardless of their sizes ,varying from 36m^2 to 450m^2, house units will include guest reception areas thought to be crucial elements of 'modern' living. In reality such areas are rarely used. Commonly missing within such designs are living areas. The spatial arrangement of the house is largely articulated as a series of enclosed rooms with minimal spatial flexibility. Cramped service areas, the laundry, the kitchen, and the servants' rooms, are always positioned at the rear part of the site. In many cases these become chaotic and unhealthy. Without any attempt to mediate the private and public space, a house is built as a walled-in solitary unit, alienating and alienated from its neighbourhood. Modern Indonesians are then obliged to reorganize how they live according to this desired 'modern' vessel.

In the 'Tomang' and 'Kebon Jeruk' house renovation projects, architect Adi Purnomo insists on reformulating aspects of spatial programming and building form. In both cases, the clients are from Jakarta's invisible middle classes. The projects are situated in a dense *kampung* neighbourhood of inner Jakarta. His design suggests a strong critique of conventional construction systems used by builders and housing estate developers in Indonesia that increasingly neglect site conditions, clients' life-style, and efficiency of spatial organization. The proposed scheme for the 'Kebon Jeruk' project is titled '*Kampung dalam Kampung*', which means a village within a village. On a long and narrow site, Purnomo creates several open courts positioned next to and across a series of enclosed room units. With this arrangement, every room has access to open air and can be spatially stretched and shrunk depending on requirements. In the 'Tomang' project, Purnomo deals with a narrower site, with two storey buildings on both sides. Here he considers privacy, natural lighting and climatic aspects. A void space is created in the middle of the building with a semi-transparent ceiling and ventilation treatment to ensure lighting quality and air circulation.

In the Ciganjur House renovation project, Purnomo deals with a more flexible space and experiments with low cost efficient building systems. On a 1000m2 site situated on the southern outskirts of Jakarta, he works with the objective of producing an efficient spatial program that minimizes wall length. Purnomo also attempts to create a fluid spatial experience dissolving the separation between interior and external spaces, where the family's living activity can be contained, developed and enriched. As in his other projects, the architect insists on working with low cost building materials in a disciplined way. This not only cuts building cost but also produces an aesthetic of subtle texture and material experience.

Rental House for City's Commuters Bintaro, Jakarta 2002–03
Architect: Andra Matin

Dealing with a different context, Andra Matin explores the possibility of providing temporary rental houses for low-income workers who live on the outskirts of Jakarta and commute to work. This widespread pattern of commuting not only contributes to the chaotic traffic jam that clogs the city in the morning and evening on a regular basis, but also reduces the life of workers to no more than working and commuting. In many cases, this condition has simply worsened the quality of life of those struggling at the lowest level of the city's economic ladder. Matin's project is situated in a village of Bintaro, next to a housing estate enclave. Matin has provided temporary accommodation where workers can stay during the week while working. He explores the possibility of creating a small yet healthy and comfortable living space with a minimal construction budget. The accommodation consists of 4 room units with a shared laundry, kitchen and toilet facility. The project makes a strong social and aesthetic statement about accommodation for low-paid workers. Around industrial areas and on the outskirts of Jakarta, low-paid workers are generally forced to live in extremely small and rudimentary shared rooms, and this project has been an insightful prototype for such dwelling units, urgently required in Jakarta.

EXPERIMENTATION WITH BUILDING MATERIALS AND CONSTRUCTION EFFICIENCY

Regardless of differences in form, size, and structural requirements, urban houses are almost always built by using concrete structural frames with cement rendered and painted brick infill walls. Despite material and cost inefficiency, this mode of building is the conventional one. Attempts to use other materials, structural systems or finishes are difficult to find because of the popularity of the cemented brick walled house, or *rumah dinding beton* as many people call it. This mode of building, unsurprisingly, is seen as 'modern' in contrast to traditional or *kampung* houses. This perception is widespread as the propaganda of the 'modern' penetrates even the most rural parts of Indonesia, despite the fact that the construction system is too expensive for most of the middle and lower class urban dwellers. For the sake of obtaining this 'modern' look, the size and quality of houses are commonly compromised.

In Bandung, architect Tan Tik Lam has developed a building system that minimizes the amount of building materials, finishing work, labour hours and maintenance. Such approaches towards building construction systems have long been used by Tan Tjiang Ay, Tik Lam's father and one of the most experienced and senior architects in Indonesia. In his numerous residential projects, Tjiang Ay insists that a functional, healthy and comfortable house can be produced on a small area of land with a very limited budget. A particular architectural aesthetic is achieved by a modest design ambition guided by a highly disciplined ethos of construction and detailing works.

In one of the most controversial recent house projects, the Steel House in eastern Jakarta, the architect Ahmad Djuhara responds to the limited finances of a middle class family by using recycled building materials – recycled steel beams and corrugated steel sheets. In the Sugiharto House project, Djuhara works within the module of these building materials, while also resolving an efficient and comfortable spatial arrangement within a small site. The cost of this house is extremely low when compared with the cost of the conventional modern house.

Steel House Jakarta 2002
Architect: Ahmad Djuhara

Through such experiments, these architects critically evaluate the given role of the profession in the last three decades within the making of the polarized urban society of Indonesia. They reject the style-driven aspirations of the 'upper' class, and insist on opening a new space of design which responds to the reality of local conditions, local neighborhood, climate, materials and construction expertise. Their works form an architecture of resistance against the projected ideal of 'modern' Indonesia.

RE-INTERPRETING THE DIALOGUE WITH THE INDIGENOUS ARCHITECTURAL TRADITION(S) AND THE TROPICAL CLIMATES

While the architecture of the 'modern' house has been launched in Indonesia, the indigenous architectural traditions have been reinterpreted simultaneously. This is problematic. If not thoroughly displaced by Western styles, indigenous traditions are largely reduced to imagery – the 'traditional' look as opposed to the 'modern'. Contemporary appropriations of indigenous traditions have in many cases been no more than the reproduction of traditional architectural ornaments in an unsatisfactory 'cut and paste' technique. This is a direct product of Suharto's cultural propaganda wherein indigenous architecture was recognized as an element of traditional(ised) culture and a precious heritage from the past. Indigenous architecture's present reality is then confined within a field of museum-isation, conservation and reproduction. The debate on how to maintain the 'unique' architectural identity of Indonesia while it undergoes rapid modernization has confused, and perhaps limited, the process of interpreting contemporary architecture in Indonesia.

A small number of architects have made attempts to reopen the debate on Indonesian architectural identity by approaching indigenous architectural traditions afresh. These architects approach proportion, climatic response and techniques of spatial articulation through the country's diverse architectural traditions. This is not an easy process. Dissuaded by essentialist and a-historical readings of Indonesian architectural languages and the banal reproductions of 'traditional' building styles, many architects chose instead to work with the minimalist, functional, and geometric language of Modernist architecture, a style in itself. With the increasing speed of communication, architects in Indonesia are very much aware of trends and contemporary issues in architecture circulated by international architectural publications. But these trends are often adopted uncritically. The decision to free oneself from the 'traditional' styles can easily end up as another form of stylistic suicide, this time by the pursuit of the formal languages of Modernist architecture.

In the Urban House (1997) project in Pamulang, Jakarta, architect Adi Purnomo incorporates lost practices of passive climatic control that were meticulously pursued in both indigenous architectural traditions and colonial Dutch-Indies architecture, particularly in the making of roof form. He suggests that, while artificial climatic controls such as air conditioning are accessible, building design should use passive climatic control by exploring roof forms and creating natural air circulation inside the house. Such climatic considerations are generally ignored by property developers, producing the typical attached row-houses where cross ventilation becomes impossible. Renovating one of these typical small house units, Purnomo built an extremely tall wall that cuts the building into two zones. The wall encloses

Urban House Jakarta 1997
Architect: Adi Purnomo

and defines an air channel, with the core of the house functioning as the centre of internal air circulation. With its striking presence, the wall disrupts the continuous roofs of the housing block, a protest against the environmentally flawed form of building rows commonly found in housing estates in the Jakarta region.

A different experiment is offered by the architect Daniel R. Sandjaja in the *Coba* (Trial) house project in Denpasar, Bali. Sandjaja explores the possibility of synthesising Modern architectural elements with techniques of spatial articulation drawn from the island's architectural traditions. Without reproducing a cliché 'Balinese' style, Sandjaja insists on reading the architectural tradition beyond its powerful appearances to work more closely with its articulation of interior and exterior space and climatic response. This is the strength of the local architectural tradition, largely overlooked in our fascination with the appearance of Balinese architecture. While the building materially and structurally resembles the currently popular minimalist-geometric architectural style, the treatments of wall enclosure and interior space speak of a careful effort to produce a fluid spatial quality and passive climatic control. The Modern tradition is not simply copied and pasted into the tropical climate, while the indigenous tradition is not reduced to exotic imagery.

Such experimentation emerging in the last five years has suggested a need to re-think the way architecture is shaped by and is shaping the emergence of modern Indonesia. These experiments have demonstrated that there are options in interpreting and positioning architecture within Indonesia's changing society. However, these projects do not constitute a radical shift or a complete resolution of the problem of contemporary inhabitation. Rather than being ideal architectural solutions totally disconnected with the near past, these projects should be read as attempts to experiment. They read about, evaluate and engage with the legacy of Suharto's regime – the polarized urban society – and the possible future, the establishment of the middle classes' mediating forces and progressive visions. It is also important to note that these architects and their critical engagements with the broader socio-cultural problem of architecture represent those on the fringe of the Indonesian architectural community.

While the country's economic crisis has instigated such experiments, the awareness of the need to build a balanced social structure for modern Indonesia is still young and vague. Necessitated mainly by the economic crisis, the sudden emergence of the urban middle class is not yet followed by the establishment of new socio-cultural roles which may mend the polarized society. Once the economic crisis subsides, such an emergence can be overcome by its near past, setting aside the new socio-cultural and architectural consciousness.[16] Architects need to realize and cultivate their role in instigating the dynamic formation of an urban middle class. The profession as a whole needs to

activate architecture as a field of experimentation which invokes conscientious modes of inhabitation, and an awareness of the changing social structure of modern Indonesia. In this way, the profession may sustain its resistance towards any attempt that seeks to conclude the ideological imagining of 'modern Indonesia'.

NOTES

1   Squatter settlements in Jakarta, the *kampungs*, despite their physical similarity are not a homogenous entity. Their diversity can be understood in terms of history of formations, ethnicities, and economic occupations. Most of the *kampungs* that occupy irregularly shaped city blocks in the centre of the city were established since from the 18th-19th century. Those that sit on the riverbanks or along the train lines and on the outskirts of the city were established since after the 1950s following the post-independence rapid migration.

2   For detailed study on the history of *kampung* culture see Lea Jellinek, *The Wheel of Fortune: The History of a Poor Community in Jakarta* (Honolulu: University of Hawaii Press, 1991) and Lea Jellinek, "Jakarta, Indonesia: Kampung Culture or Consumer Culture?" in *Consuming Cities: The Urban Environment in the Global Economy after the Rio Declaration*, eds., Nicholas Low, Brendan Gleeson, Ingemar Elander, Rolf Lidskog (London: Routledge, 2000): 265-280.

3   See H. Akihary, *Ir. F.J.L. Ghijsels: Architect in Indonesia (1910–1929)* (Utrecht: Seram Press, 1996): 98-100 and Aditya W. Fitrianto, "Real Estat Menteng dalam Dilema," *Kompas* (11 August 2002).

4   For further discussion on Dutch Indies architecture see Helen Jessup, *Netherlands Architecture in Indonesia, 1900–1942*, PhD dissertation Courtauld Institute of Art (University of London, 1989).

5   See Susan Abeyasekere, ed., *From Batavia to Jakarta: Indonesia's Capital 1930s to 1980s* (Monash University: 1985): 2, and Achmad D. Tardiyana, "Persoalan Pemugaran Kawasan Dalam Pembangunan Kota," *Kompas* (12 August 2001).

6   The Dutch Colonial Government, necessitated by the introduction of the "Colonial Ethical Policy" in the late 1920s, undertook a small scale of kampung improvement project. Architect and planner Thomas Karsten was assigned to analyze the problems of Kampung, see Abidin Kusno, *Behind the Postcolonial: Architecture, Urban Space and Political Cultures in Indonesia* (London: Routledge, 2000): 128–133. See also Wertheim, W.F. et al (eds), "The Indonesian Town," in *Koninklijk Instituut voor de Tropen* (The Hague: W. van Hoeve Ltd., 1958).

Since the early 1980s, a number of kampung improvement projects and public housing projects, mainly proposed and operated as community based developments, emerged in urban centers centres in Java, such as the works of the late planner Hasan Poerbo, the late architect and religious leader Romo Mangunwijaya, the architect Andy Siswanto, and *Perumnas* (National Housing Board). Among these projects are Kali Code in Yogyakarta; Cengkareng, Penjaringan, and Sunter public housings in Jakarta; and Banjarhardjo in Semarang.

7   Kusno, *Behind the Postcolonial*, 71-166.

8   Benedict Anderson introduces the term "imagined community" to convey his argument that the notion of nation is imagined, constructed, and authorized to maintain a certain desired power relation. See Benedict Anderson, *Imagined Communities: Reflections on the Origin and Spread of Nationalism* (London: Verso, 1991). In his subsequent study, Anderson examines the way Suharto's New Order regime re-imagined the nation after taking over the ruling of the country from Sukarno. Here Anderson traces the transformation from revolutionary Indonesia into the military authoritarian New Order Indonesia. See Benedict Anderson, *Language and Power: Exploring Political Cultures in Indonesia* (Ithaca: Cornell University Press, 1990).

9   See Michael Leaf, "The Suburbanisation of Jakarta: a Concurrence of Economics and Ideology," in Third World Planning Review, 16, 4: 343-56 and Kusno, *Behind the Postcolonial*, 113.

10 Ariel Heryanto, "Agenda Studi Kebudayaan," in *Perlawanan dalam Kepatuhan: Esai-Esai Budaya Ariel Heryanto*, ed. Idi Subandy Ibrahim (Bandung: Mizan, 2000): 59–63.

11 See Kusno, *Behind the Postcolonial*, 109–119.

12 Until recently, the discussion on middle class Indonesia has been vague and unsatisfactory. The significance of middle classes formation in Indonesia has never been questioned, instigated or duly recognized. Recent studies have emerged and provided insightful analysis on this issue, see Ariel Heryanto, "Public Intellectuals, Media, and Democratization: Cultural Politics of the Middle Classes in Indonesia," in *Challenging Authoritarianism in Southeast Asia*, eds. Ariel Heryanto and Sumit K. Mandal (London: RoutledgeCurzon, 2003): 24–59. See also other essays in this book.

13 Among these exclusive estates is *Pondok Indah* (Beautiful Hut), which was modelled on the Beverly Hills housing images, and the recently built Kota Wisata (Travelling City) where one can choose to live in the "Japanese quarter", "Paris quarter", or other regional quarters. For an analysis on the growing popularity of 'first world' architectural styles see Saya Shiraishi, "Silahkan Masuk, Silahkan Duduk: Reflections in a Sitting Room in Java," Indonesia, 41:89–130.

14 Further elaboration on the history of Jakarta and the marginalization of the kampung can be found in Susan Abeyasekere, *Jakarta: A History* (Singapore: Oxford University Press, 1987) and Michael Leaf, *Land Regulation and Housing Development in Jakarta, Indonesia: From the 'Big Village' to the 'Modern City'*, PhD Dissertation (University of California at Berkeley, USA, 1991).

15 For an examination on of the spatial effects of the 1998 riots and the subsequent reappearance of "Chinese Cultures" see Abidin Kusno, "Remembering/Forgetting the May Riots: Architecture, Violence, and the Making of "Chinese Cultures" in Post-1998 Jakarta," in *Public Culture*, 15(1): 149–177 (Duke University Press).

16 Just recently, an article appeared in the national newspaper describing a re-emerging demand for a Neo Classical architectural style in the making of urban houses in Jakarta. The article reports how architects and clients in Jakarta have learnt to adjust their dream of the Neo-Classical building style within the ongoing economic crisis by adapting the style into a smaller scale building, contrasted with its former extravagant trendsetter, the *Pondok Indah* housing estate. See Robert Adhi KSP, "Rumah, Kembali ke Gaya Neoklasik," *Kompas* (25 April 2003).

Jakarta 2003

RECENT THAI HOUSES: DIVERSITY WITHOUT INTEGRATION

BY PIRAK ANURAKYAWACHON

Pirak Anurakyawachon is a contributing editor to art4d magazine. He studied architecture at Silpakorn University, Bangkok and has practised as an architect in Europe and the USA.

"Thai architecture is dead!"... A plaintive cry from Associate Professor Somchart Chungsiriarak conveys the frustration and the uncertainty facing Thai architects at the beginning of the 21st Century. The economic crash, the faltering love affair with American culture, and the conflict between traditional Thai architecture and globalized Western architecture have led to confusion. Chaos and diversity are paramount, with an architectural present that views its own past in a blinding light of contradiction and complexity.

In 1997, the Thai economic bubble burst and architects were conspicuous casualties. Thailand's massive foreign debt had been largely fuelled by the excesses of the speculative property market in Bangkok, and when the economy crashed, local architects were forced to look for other work. Some became chefs, some became movie stars, some turned to interior design and graphic design, but some jumped back to university and turned to theory.

The cessation of building work gave architects the time to retreat, realize and to reconsider the reality. Architects have subsequently addressed issues of meaning, technology and sustainability. Many wondered how and why they had designed the ugly eclectic buildings of the property boom. The skyline of Bangkok is testament to the failure of the economy and the false ambitions of the architects. Unfinished skyscrapers litter the landscape, and the style of these now ironic monuments reflects the intellectual paucity of the architects. Many (even mature) architects got the opportunity to design, but they just closed their eyes and made a sketch. And the sketch was built. Now maybe three or four architects compete to design one house, so the house is now the great opportunity to realize their potential. Ten years ago, these architects would never have looked at a house.

Since the end of World War II, Thai economic and political survival has been dependent on America. The USA strategically utilized Thailand as a buffer against communism spreading through Asia from China, and Thailand was the base for American operations in the Vietnam War. The Thai economy was kept afloat through American aid, and of course by the spectacular amounts of money spent by American servicemen on their R 'n' R activities. This essentially false and sleazy/glamorous period of American lifestyle forever altered Thai culture and Thai politics. American 'pop' culture from the 1960s has remained part of Thailand's aesthetic, despite the American withdrawal from the region in the 1970s. The ongoing fascination with the Coca-Cola type of image can be seen in the artefacts which adorn Lubid Studio (2002), by Karn Boontarik. The artworks are an amusing and crazy collection of iconic American themes from the days of Elvis Presley and the Mickey Mouse Club. The house itself is a much heavier version of the California Case Study Houses, which were built just after World War II. The Lubid Studio points to a delightful re-engagement between Thai culture and American culture. It could symbolize the possibility for Bangkok to be an architectural crazy city, and capitalize on the colourful meetings between East and West.

An apocryphal story in the course of modern Thai architecture relates to the visit of Walter Gropius in 1953. Architecture students took the great Modernist architect to look at a new house, which had been built in a traditional area with a riverbank lifestyle. The new house was built with steel material that had been imported from abroad, and the surrounding houses were built from thatch. Gropius asked why only one house was built from steel with zinc roofing

Lubid Studio Bangkok 2002 >
Architect: Karn Boontarik

panels. The students replied that this was a house for rich people, and that the others were for the poor. The founder of the Bauhaus and the champion of Modernism then said that he preferred the houses of the poor people because the architecture was so beautiful and charming.

Traditional Thai architecture is adorned with fabulous decorative ornamentation, which respects a connection with the spirits. This is a representation of an ideological relationship between the tangible world and the heavenly powers. This relationship in Thai architecture is a legacy from the Khmer period of the eleventh and twelfth centuries. The most beautiful period in Thai architectural history was the Sukhothai era from the thirteenth to the fifteenth centuries. The tapering *chedi* or *stupa* was the architectural symbol of this period, which also produced the most elegant Buddha sculptures. Palaces and temples throughout Thailand demonstrate most clearly this sculptural representation of spiritual belief. Physically, the Thai house was always intended to provide a peaceful atmosphere, and this was created by a process and method of planning and building that we now characterize as vernacular. Prefabricated panels are supported by a robust framework of columns, and wooden pegs are used instead of nails. The wisdom of Thai craftsmen is manifest in the expedient construction techniques. By tradition, a house in a Thai village must be built within one day, so collective labour is used. The Thai house could then be dismantled, moved and reassembled in one day. Different areas of Thailand had different style of decoration, and all Thai houses have their own 'spirit house' which often resembles a dolls house replica of a beautiful temple. The traditional Thai house can be categorized as a one-storey residential structure on an elevated platform above an open ground level known as the 'Tai Toon' which provides ventilation and protection from floods. Most Thai people live on lowlands, which are prone to frequent flooding. The distinctive formal characteristics of the Thai house are steep roofs with long slender eaves, wide verandahs and tall windows with low sills.

Foreign architects were first commissioned to design in Thailand during the reign of King Rama IV (1851-1868), and this is when the Western influence is first noted. Western lifestyle infiltrated social, political and cultural aspects of life in Thailand. The foreign architects adapted their own methods to suit local climatic conditions and the local context. This 'imported' architecture interpreted traditional Thai architectural language, and is regarded as very successful. The 'Pan Yah' or 'Manila' type of house which evolved during the reign of King Rama V (1868–1910) was overtly concerned with air circulation within the house, and the house was artfully located at the centre of a broad green lawn. The distinctive fretwork decoration beneath the eaves has resulted in these houses being affectionately known as 'gingerbread houses' due to their resemblance of the packaging of imported gingerbread. This period leading into the early 20th Century can be seen as the time when authentic and original Thai domestic architecture faded away. Many eclectic styles emerged with a blending of South Chinese and Portuguese. These styles mirrored the colonial architecture, which was so well known in Malaysia and Singapore. A direct descendant of this type of house is Vit Vattanayothin's House (2002) by Boonlert Hemvijitraphran. This is a graceful house in a colonial style, though built from steel rather than wood and masonry. The elegant white 'mansion' also reverts to the picturesque placement within a green lawn, and the ensemble re-introduces the harmonious composition which distinguished colonial architecture.

The history of Thai architecture in the 20th Century has seen many instances of architects straining to incorporate a Thai sensibility in their work. The simplistic reading of results of this process has been the application of Thai decoration and motifs to the facades of modern buildings. This view of recent approaches masks the complexities of a true search for an authentic Thai architecture, but this search will not emerge from an appropriation of soaring gable roofs or carved wooden lintels. In the lengthy course of Thai history, it must come from a re-examination of the architectural and artistic values which represented a spiritual connection between the earth and the heavens. This understanding is currently very ambiguous as globalization subverts traditional Thai cultural values. Advertisements now proclaim that your house tells the world who you are, but the irony is that your 'individual' house is identical to hundreds

Vit Vattanayothin House Bangkok 2002 >
Architect: Boonlert Hemvijitraphran

Rujinarong's House Bangkok 2003
Architect: Tinakorn Rujinarong

of others. In the embrace of the consumer society, the 'house' has become just another badge for the owner's status, which seems to be enhanced further with the application of Western architectural elements. The notorious 'monster houses' have replaced decorum and good taste. If research was to be carried out on domestic Thai architecture, it could be revealing as to whether these 'monster houses' are peaceful houses or angry houses. Traditional Thai houses were specifically intended to promote a peaceful atmosphere, and it is possible to suspect that this intention may have disappeared. Tinakorn Rujinarong's own house (2003) was deliberately designed to be peaceful. Rujinarong has taken the minimalist precedents of early Le Corbusier and the New York Whites to create a tranquil haven. Perhaps this can be seen as an honest and perceptive approach to reintroducing spiritual values to the Thai house, as Rujinarong borrows the intent rather than the method.

As the economy recovers, and it now appears to be nearly back in boom time, residential and renovation projects are the main workplace for architects. The government has lowered interest rates to encourage the potential house owner to spend, and it is to be hoped that an intelligent application of values learned from the 1997 crash will be perceived. But nobody can say what the Thai 'House for the

21st Century' will be. Speaking at the ARCASIA Forum 11 in 2001, Kanika Ratanapridakul[1] asked direct and provocative questions of the architectural profession in its relationship and usefulness to society...

"For those of who may not be aware, the search of Thai-ness in the contemporary architectural scene in Thailand has been a hot pursuit for many Thai architects since the day of globalization. The general feeling is that the effect of the globalize economy and Western dominate mass media had progressively contaminated and eradicated the 'Thai-ness' in every respects of Thai cultures. And architecture received no exception. My feeling is that this cultural crisis of ours stemmed from the fact that our history lessons failed to install the sense of gratitude towards the past in our children and our education as a whole failed to improve the general level of intellect of our people. In short, we have failed to prepare our people to deal with the complexity of globalization.... I don't view our identity as being lost but rather drastically transformed – so drastic that it can often become very difficult to identify or recognize. And though one's identity is never there to be found or discovered but it emerges, genuine and unpretentious, through understanding of history and culture day by day. And also must be a comprehension in the values, not the result. Otherwise, it will be just and applying a formal code, while betraying the real intention."

The litmus test for Thai cultural reassertion is the great city of Bangkok, a metropolitan area that is so much larger than any other in Thailand. This relationship between a city and its country has no equivalent internationally, apart from city-states. The population of Bangkok is at least 10 million, and it is more than 40 times more populous than Chiang Mai, the next largest city. Bangkok has both a practical power and an invisible pull over the rest of the country. It is a city of dominant typologies and vertical vistas, a heaving battleground of urban growth and mutation. The congestion and chaos is visual, cerebral, aural and architectural. The streets of the city provide fragmented views of skytrains, expressways, derelict skyscrapers, hotels, concrete apartment towers, street-stalls, red-light areas, and constant vertical

Sukhumvit Road Bangkok 2003

rhythms of brightly colored signs and lights. The movement of this city and the multi-layered structures of complexity must inspire a culture and an architecture that can have a real dynamism. It has happened in Tokyo, surely it can happen here. The hyper-potentiality of the urban fabric must be a fertile ground for an exciting architecture for urban living.

Thai architecture is not dead, but it will be fascinating to view its awakening from a troubled sleep. The four Thai houses featured in this book may just be the precedents for houses that will reclaim a position which is defiantly Thai. The architects must discover some new directions with innovation and provocation, as long as they know and believe in what they are doing. And then one day, in the near future, we can proudly say... "This is a Thai house".

NOTES

1   Kanika Ratanapridakul *ARCASIA, Forum 11*, Singapore 6 September 2001

BEYOND THE VERNACULAR HOUSE

BY ANOMA PIERIS

Anoma Pieris has degrees from the University of Moratuwa, Sri Lanka and the Massachusetts Institute of Technology. She has practiced as an architect in Sri Lanka and in Singapore.

Traditionally, the rural dwelling in South Asia (here defined as India and Sri Lanka) has been a sleeping place with its activities unravelling into the surrounding landscape. In a village community there are no boundaries between houses. Open-air activities include farming, cooking, the care of animals, tending to market gardens and bathing or washing at a communal well. The concept of the house as an individuated unit within a fenced compound, and property ownership by a nuclear family, suggested affluence and colonial habits, where communal priorities were abandoned for a more private value system. In the late 18th Century the rural dwelling was transformed in order to accommodate colonial priorities, and was constructed with permanent materials such as brick and mortar with tiled roofs. Anthony King, writing on the Anglo Indian Bungalow, traces its origins to the Bengali peasant hut (Bangla) with its sloping thatched roof and gable ends.[1] Such associations are seen to have proliferated throughout Britain's Indian 'possessions' from the late 18th Century onwards. The need to adapt to a dry or humid climate and extreme heat provoked particular attention to climate in house design. The relationship between the individuated colonial bungalow and the communal character of vernacular building articulated societal tensions both racial and structural.

Modernisation and the resultant introversion of family life carried the domestic house in South Asia far from communal interests into new and alien ways of dwelling, heralding the birth of the middle classes. Separate dwelling expresses the new identity learned through citizenship and the nuclear family unit that was created by South Asia's independence. Post-colonial South Asia is bound by hybrid priorities where Western aspirations are strained through local cultural filters. Cricket, Bollywood, religion, a rich culinary tradition and a more recent involvement with the global high-tech industry are flanked by a strong and vocal (often violent) political culture. In an unstable economic climate, where popular choices remain a sensitive register of political attitudes, the house is a primary site through which historical and social change can be evaluated. The penetration of modern urban stylings provokes a new form of dwelling, modelled on Western space requirements but adapted to South Asian cultural traditions and behaviours. Although South Asian architecture often retains the raised plinth or the projecting verandahs of rural models, the dark interiors, communal sleeping spaces and external service areas are no longer considered desirable. As middle class aspirations demand greater proportions of private and personal space, the imperatives of the modern house become the very antithesis of rural architecture. Nevertheless, due to the urgent desire to re-affirm geographic belonging in local post-independence architectural practice, some of the best examples of residential design in South Asia are inspired by the vernacular.

Reorientation towards local architecture in India has colonial beginnings in the Hindu, Islamic or Buddhist style architecture designed by such as Lutyens, Herbert Baker and Chisholm. Their efforts to include religious motifs and to design for climatic sensibilities can be considered the first attempts at a regionalist public architecture. Similarly South Asian cultural nationalists during the 1930s and 1940s borrowed from the Arts and Crafts legacy of Britain and applied its ideas to the revival of local craft. In architecture, they drew attention to both historic and regional examples as possible sources of inspiration.[2] However, 'tradition'

Chennai India 2003

provided a limited palette for the aspirations of a newly independent India, and progress needed to be articulated in a modern idiom. In the post war years, under the patronage of Prime Minister Nehru, European Modernism took centre stage as the appropriate architectural expression to project India's modern self-definition to the rest of the world. The new Punjabi capital, Chandigarh, brought Le Corbusier to India along with Pierre Jeanneret, Maxwell Fry and Jane Drew. Each attempted the difficult resolution of reinterpreting modern ideologies through communal needs within a framework of global expectations. Louis Kahn built first in Ahmadabad during the 1960s and later designed the Parliament House in Dacca, Bangladesh, while Joseph Allen Stein and Laurie Baker took residence in India and produced a more local architecture. While these architects failed to seduce Indian architecture into a Modernist vocabulary, they inspired a more self-conscious approach to design that drove South Asian architects to seriously reconsider the 'vernacular'.

The work of South Asian architects after Chandigarh was originally disseminated through the *Mimar* publication series, which concentrated on regional, Islamic, non–Western architecture. Its orientation towards community projects and emphasis on regional design, focused attention on vernacular derived architecture. In the liberal arts, the vernacular had been revisited as a democratic position that foregrounded place-based identities which needed to be addressed after the colonial period. The vernacular as a direct response to a local building tradition and climate was seen as an appropriate and inclusive expression of geographic belonging, which could appeal to the sensibilities of the largely rural indigenous population. Architecture was thus seen to be playing a significant role in the reconstruction of national identity. 'Regionalism' was presented as a position resistant to the International Style of foreign architects, and for the first time gave international visibility to the work of South Asian practitioners. Writers such as Tzonis and Lefaivre, and Kenneth Frampton, helped establish this regional approach as a mainstream movement against which subsequent Asian architectures could be evaluated.[3] The 'new-vernacular' responded to the conditions of the site, the material and textural attributes of regional

models, construction methods and craftsmanship in order to build an architecture that was considered more appropriate to the context than the prevailing trend of international Modernism. Cumulatively these approaches established a value system that was centred upon genius loci and more importantly, brought local architects in India such as Charles Correa, Raj Rawal and Balakrishna Doshi, as well as Geoffrey Bawa in Sri Lanka, to prominence. Where a previous generation had been enamoured of European styles, there was a new impetus to break away from European and American examples in search of a local idiom.

Chennai India 2003

UNDERSTANDING THE VERNACULAR

One of the major problems encountered in the revival of vernacular architecture has been its dislocation from a rural context, and its transformation into an elite architectural expression. This displacement, with imagery which borrows from the British picturesque tradition, attempts to make a designed artefact or landscape appear natural. Moreover, the rustic architecture of rural life needs to be modified in scale, and its services need to be upgraded before it can satisfy urban middle or upper-class aspirations. In the process of this transformation, the original spirit of vernacular architecture and the simple life to which it alludes may be compromised, even as its image becomes increasingly popular.

To understand the vernacular without reducing it to a pre-modern or nativist category requires an appreciation of the moral economy inherent in its conception. If compared with examples in the United States, it is found not in the individualism of Henry Thoreau, but in the puritanism of groups like the Shakers. In order to *design* the vernacular within its own frame, as a communal architectural type, it becomes necessary to abandon a concept central to the idea of home ownership – the individual householder. 'Sustainable environments' that are energy efficient and self-reliant often flourish in alternative definitions of community, where the greater common good of a group of people and their particular way of life stands as the ideal. Such communities choose not to acquire the social or cultural capital created by material accumulation, and live on the margins of mainstream economic life. Architects who embrace this approach to house and home typically operate on limited budgets, and often reflect philosophies that separate them from the outside world.

An understanding of the vernacular can do little more than establish the starting point for a discussion of regionalism. A particular context may gain its regional identity by the replication of a building type as a series. Often this identity reflects the terrain, climate, materials and construction methods of that region. The pragmatism of using available materials and methods often draws vernacular building types into discussions of sustainable architecture. Although the term 'sustainable architecture' suggests ecological and environmentally sensitive design, and is typically found in the ad-hoc pragmatism of alternative communities or the technologically sophisticated work of First World practitioners, it is an approach often exemplified in vernacular dwellings. Auroville, in South India, is unusual in this regard as it attracts both local and international architects intent on creating sustainable architecture. Following the regional legacy and communal focus of architects such as Laurie Baker, these practitioners refuse to yield to the aesthetic seduction of the vernacular as a picturesque image.[4] In Auroville the traditions and methods of local village building are being modified in order to build more substantial villages. The moral economy of the local vernacular becomes apparent as a rigorous approach towards communal housing, generating modular units of production and cost-saving construction methods.

AUROVILLE

Auroville is situated a few miles outside the Sri Aurobindo Ashram, a religious community established in Pondicherry by Sri Aurobindo (Aravind Ghose 1872–1950), India's nationalist intellectual. It is the vision of the founder saint and his devotee Mirra Alfasa (1878–1973) also known as 'The Mother', who created an environment unique for its denial of the hierarchies which often atomise ashram environments. Due to the horizontal comradeship envisioned by Sri Aurobindo, the on-going project to construct the city of Auroville has attracted live-in architects from all over the world, and has created a platform for experimental technologies and sustainable environments. For example, Antonin Raymond, best known for his Modernist legacy in Japan, and the furniture designer George Nakashima are among those whose desire to integrate private and professional life led to their contribution to the ashram's architecture. If there is such a thing as a utopian city, Auroville aspires to become one when it fulfils its initial urban plan by 2025. Similar to Paolo Soleri's Arcosanti in the Arizona desert, the city is an experiment in sustainability with a range of activities including: 'afforestation, organic agriculture, educational research, health care, village development, appropriate technology, ... town planning,

Brickmaking Auroville, India

water table management, cultural activities and community services'. Whereas many ashrams in other parts of India function as gated communities intent on attracting spiritual seekers from the West, Auroville is surrounded by and interspersed with local villages. The ashram's adherents practice a form of integral yoga where they surrender self-interest and manifest their faith through karma or 'work'. Unlike ashrams in most parts of India, there are no prescriptive gender roles, and women are among Auroville's most prominent practitioners.

The landscape of Auroville is red – from the rich earth that is used in brick making, and from the clay for the earthenware pots and clay ovens. Apart from the bricks, roof tiles, floor tiles and grills, the raised floors are made from this red earth, giving the impression that the buildings of this nascent city are literally born of its landscape. This kinship between the landscape and the dwelling space, which is a cogent metaphor for sustainability, is an important attribute of Auroville's architectural program. The architecture is simple and pragmatic, utilising low cost technologies and

< Anupama Kundoo House Auroville, India 1999
Architect: Anupama Kundoo

depends largely on local materials and construction methods. Although often quite unlike the traditional rural buildings, the basic dwelling unit can be considered a test case for the moral economy upon which the ideals of vernacular regional architectures are founded. If we take a look at the houses built by volunteer architects for themselves in Auroville, we find that the new technologies borrow and build on the rural architecture of Pondicherry, which surrounds and penetrates its vast acreage. The architect-designed buildings standardise these same technologies, and introduce innovative materials and methods to enable their large-scale utilisation.

Upon entering the Auroville community, an architect's first task is to build their own residence. They may begin building at a small scale, perhaps using temporary materials, but expand it later with greater confidence and permanence. These houses provide prototypes of small-scale experimental dwellings which can be adapted by rural communities. In larger projects such as communal kitchens, schools and offices, site-work commences with a large quantity of red earth dug up on site for adobe brick construction. Using material found on the site eliminates transportation costs, while the pit that remains after the earth is removed is used for the treatment of sewage by perma-culture. The sewage is filtered through a series of ponds that have been turned into water gardens. Adobe bricks are hand compacted and sun dried or fired. The traditional fired brick is both decorative and easy to corbel and to handle.

Although we can see the influence of architects like Laurie Baker, Louis Kahn and Le Corbusier in Auroville's geometric forms and light-filled volumes, the houses are constructed through the innovative adaptation of inexpensive local materials. By their example, they push the limits of vernacular construction methods by adapting them to modern programs. Since Auroville applies both modern and traditional technologies that are easily transferable to the surrounding village buildings, it enables the integration of new building methods for rural development. Labour for all the work comes from surrounding villages, providing employment between agricultural seasons – an advantage of the ashram concept is that it is already embedded within the local religious and cultural tradition. Architecture is not

merely a relationship between an architect and a client. It involves responsibilities to the culture of local practice, and to labour and the social context beyond the specific building envelope. Indeed, the undeniable value of the vernacular approach is in its expression of 'a way of building' i.e. process as well as method, as more important than the aesthetic or picturesque achievements of product-oriented architecture.

DEFINING SRI LANKAN MODERNITY

The difficult journey, away from the moral economy of a rural livelihood in search of a modern economic life is best expressed in the transformation of vernacular architecture into a modern aesthetic. In appropriating the vernacular tradition, South Asian architects have attempted to resolve the tension between the values associated with vernacular architecture and the modern aspirations that seek to transform them. The product is often a compromise between Eastern needs and Western desires. The architecture of Sri Lanka, an island nation at the southern tip of India, best describes this predicament. Due to its small size and compact communities, Sri Lanka has proved to be an exemplary template for the generation of a designed vernacular. While it paralleled India in its colonial architectural relationships, it differed in one respect – its most significant experiments occurred in domestic architecture. Sri Lanka's public architecture although noteworthy, has an independent history with each subsequent coloniser (Portuguese, Dutch and British) leaving their mark. Close on independence in 1948 the British helped evolve a Sinhala-Buddhist style architecture, which was later appropriated for an ethno-centric political nationalism. During the 1950s and 1960s the 'traditionalism' practised by the state provoked an opposite architectural resistance from its citizens. Urban dwellers expressed their independence from colonial rule by redefining ways of life, speech, every-day habits and dwelling spaces through modern rather than traditional aspirations.

In the years following independence, the house escaped the dark introverted interiors of the colonial bungalow and the traditional wattle and daub constructions to let light, that modern element, into the heart of its private spaces. The verandah with all its airiness and colour entered the house and encouraged private lives to look outside. This radical transformation, and its attendant awareness of space and form, suggested that the intimate lives of Sri Lankans had re-entered public space, and independence was being claimed by an emerging modern polity on their own terms. In the absence of a local alternative this transformation was achieved by a new residential impetus from America's Pacific Coast that was disseminated through a burgeoning magazine culture. The 1950s and 1960s saw the rapidly rising middle-class conduct their first tentative experiments with architectural Modernism. The 'American Style', an architecture associated with modern suburban life, proved to be a universal phenomenon spreading from Monsieur Hulot's Paris to the new industrial cities of Asia, leaving an uncertain, and sometimes unwelcome, legacy of haphazard innovation.[5] Split levels, textured walls and large areas of glazing looking out on to the terrace and the garden broke up box-like rooms that had once segregated hierarchies of race, class and gender. 'The American Style' fulfilled two needs. First, the necessity to break away from all things 'British Colonial', and second, the desire to break out into an extroverted flexible living environment. It was this break that enabled the first cautious attempts at self-definition.

PIONEERING EFFORTS

The copybook mimicry of 'American Style' architecture provoked a reactionary response during the late 1960s by a class of architects who argued the need for a regionally-derived Modern architecture. Just as the Impressionists of turn-of-the century Europe had turned to everyday life for inspiration, the art and literature in post-independence Sri Lanka focused on village life as a primary subject, breaking away from Colonial traditions. During the late 1960s and 1970s the vernacular proved a non-partisan response to a political contradiction, Sri Lanka's desire to be both authentic (i.e. traditional) and progressive (i.e. modern) without stoking the fires of rising ethno-centric religious nationalism. This impossible combination of expectations was resolved by reiterating seemingly Modernist tenets such as 'a way of

building', respecting the site and responding to the climate. The careful avoidance of religious or royalist styles confirmed the secular democratic urge of this architectural position. Courtyards, verandahs and pitched roofs were reintroduced into urban space, and the first generation of local architects in Sri Lanka established their careers through their passion for studying vernacular architecture.

Sri Lankan architecture has three mentors who have taken a very different approach towards architecture. Minette de Silva, the 'grande dame' of South Asian architecture, focused on deriving space from social agendas and facilitating the socialising process most familiar to the culture.[6] Her houses were designed to accommodate and enhance festivals, weddings and funerals; the ways in which the extended family gathered together; and the preparation of food and the rituals of a religiously entrenched culture. She used forms and materials that were influenced by kilns, paddy storage structures and the rich craftsmanship of the Kandyan region where she executed much of her work. Valentine Gunasekara, perhaps the least publicised of the three, was captivated by the tectonic and innovative possibilities of Modernist form, light, and materials. His interest in engineering and structural expression inspired a redefinition of modern spatial experiences for the society and context. The spatial celebration of family life remained central to his experiments. Geoffrey Bawa, who has been the most

Illangakoon House Rosemead Place, Colombo 1969–71
Architect: Valentine Gunasekara

frequently publicized of the three, recreated vernacular architectural experiences with a keen eye for the picturesque possibilities of framed views and formally choreographed movement. His architecture borrowed liberally from the natural beauty of its tropical setting which remained the focus of many of his spatial experiences. It sowed the first seeds of a tourist industry that romanticised the scenographic possibilities of the tropical landscape, and revived the colonial habits and leisure concomitant with their appreciation.

All three of these architects practised through a strictly socialist political and economic regime which prohibited the importation of building materials and forced a dependence on local materials and methods. Consequently their architecture strayed far from the Cartesian forms of Modernism to produce additive informal organisations of space, and utilized textured, often natural, surfaces. Bawa, who was the most successful in adapting the vernacular, became the most influential of the three and educated the next generation to his 'way of building' which suited the shrinking budgets of most Sri Lankans at the time. Perhaps the most important feature of Bawa's architecture was achieved through his use of the pitched tiled roof-form as a generative device provoking multiple courtyard spaces. His approach, which prompted the design of houses using the roof plan as a guide, invoked its own particular spatial ordering system.

THE NEW VERNACULAR

After Bawa's example, and often under his mentor-ship, many architects including Ashley De Vos, Ismeth Raheem and Feroze Choksy, Mihindu Keertiratne, Anura Ratnavibushana and C Anjalendran, embraced the vernacular derivative until it became the norm for both private and public architecture. This style reached its zenith in Bawa's New University at Ruhuna and in the Sri Lankan Parliament. *Mimar* (the journal published under the auspices of the Aga Khan) once again became the voice of this vernacular sensibility, which now ranged from low-cost housing to monumental architecture. At its best it helped construct a

National Parliament Kotte, Sri Lanka 1979–82
Architect: Geoffrey Bawa

strong regional identity that influenced both South and Southeast Asian architectural practice and gave international recognition to local geographies on their own terms. To local practitioners it held out the promise of autonomy from Euro-centric paradigms in the evaluation of regional architectures. At its worst it was commodified as a representation of past traditions.

With the re-emergence of Sri Lanka into a capitalist economic culture during the late 1970s, the vernacular offered thematic possibilities that were stretched to meet a range of programs including multi-storey structures. As its scope expanded in scale it began to feed a burgeoning tourist industry that targeted Westerners. Both Bawa and the second generation of Sri Lankan architects contributed to this trend, and vernacular-derived hotel architecture proliferated. The house was magnified and multiplied a hundred-fold into a vast hospitality landscape that strove to provide local domesticity and colonial traditions of service to Western clients. Punctuated by the political and economic seesaw that held Sri Lankans in thrall, the progress of vernacular-derived architecture was gradually transformed into an elite style of life, accessible to few Sri Lankans. At its peak during the 1980s and 1990s, as the house grew in scale into vast domestic complexes it became conflated with the *Walawwa* or the elite houses of feudal ancestors. Its spaces multiplied

Pettah Colombo, Sri Lanka 2003

technology in every-day life has precipitated a revival of a long forestalled experiment with Modernism. In the work of the architects selected here, we see many of the traces of their previous legacy of courtyards, the play of interior light and the richness of texture. The introversion of building space in many of these examples responds to the increasing desire for security precipitated by a volatile political environment. It simultaneously reflects the failure of building regulation to build community space respecting reciprocal street identities at a local level. Indeed the proliferation of private spaces is pervasive in this new generation of houses.

The three architects shown in this book can be set apart from their equivalents in Southeast Asia in their desire for textured surfaces and vibrant colours that are often rejected by Southeast Asian minimalism. Their projects are not limited to an elite clientele but are to be found in Colombo's outlying suburbs. They look beyond the picturesque to alternative expressions of everyday life for modern Sri Lankans.

NOTES

1 Anthony D.King, *The bungalow : the production of a global culture*, London ; Boston : Routledge & Kegan Paul, 1984.

2 For example Ananda K.Coomaraswamy, in his *The Manifesto of the Ceylon Social Reform Society*, p5, put forward views that were influenced by the Arts and Crafts Movement in London.

3 See, Kenneth Frampton, Towards a Critical Regionalism: Six Points Towards an Architecture of Resistance, Hal Foster edition *The Anti Aesthetic: Essays on Post Modern Culture*, Port Townsend Wash: Bay Press 1983; Alexander Tzonis and Liane Lefaivre, Towards a non-oppressive environment; an essay, Boston, i Press; distributed by G. Braziller, New York, 1972.

Alexander Tzonis, Liane Lefaivre and Bruno Stagno ed.s *Tropical architecture : critical regionalism in the age of globalization*, Chichester : Wiley, 2001.

4 See, Gautam Bhatia, *Laurie Baker: Life, Work, Writings*, Viking/Hudco, 1991, p15 & p39.

5 In the film 'Mon Oncle' directed by Jacques Tati in 1958, the stage set is a modern California-style house

6 Minnette de Silva, Experiments in Modern Regional Architecture in Ceylon: 1950–1960, *(Journal of Ceylon Institute of Architects, 1965/66*, p13)

into numerous verandahs, courtyards and living rooms, which once again introduced systems of segregation. The legacy of flowing spaces borrowed from Modernism and the American Style was lost in the proliferation of contained environments. The maintenance of modern comfort levels in rustic environments ultimately required an excess of labour.

LOOKING BEYOND VERNACULAR ARCHITECTURE

Once again architects in Sri Lanka have had to seek a new architectural resolution, to cope with a modern, potentially stressful servant-less existence. Increased reliance on

St Lucia House Brisbane, Australia 1999
Architect: Peter Skinner and Elizabeth Watson-Brown

AN ONGOING PREOCCUPATION: AUSTRALIA AND THE SMALL HOUSE

BY PHILIP GOAD

Philip Goad is Professor of Architecture and Deputy Dean of the Faculty of Architecture, Building and Planning at The University of Melbourne.

In 1952, architect and critic Robin Boyd declared with sweeping confidence that "Australia is the small house".[1] Fifty years later one can make the same generalisation and one might be (like Boyd), only half accurate. Boyd had coined the phrase to highlight the subject of *Australia's Home*, his seminal history of house design in Australia – an account of the progressive 'bungalow-isation' of the everyday house from the 1830s to the 1950s. It was a damning and biased account of the typical suburban house, and was intended to be read as a polemic for modernist reform. Boyd outlined the typology of the Australian house as it had developed and the complacent middle class taste that had created it. His book suggested that serious experiment in domestic design was urgently required. And throughout the 1950s and 1960s, many Australian architects responded to this suggestion. Houses designed by architects such as the European émigrés Harry Seidler and Hugh Buhrich in New South Wales, Geoffrey Summerhayes in Perth, Peter Heathwood in Queensland, and Boyd himself in Victoria were inventive, sometimes tiny, even cranky pieces of architectural research.[2] They were houses that questioned fundamental issues such as the conventional house plan, the form of the roof as a delineator of volume or its ability to provide free planning beneath, the skin of the house as a climate mediator, or the ability to live virtually outdoors. For the brave client, these were houses that put new ways of living to the test, to inspire future generations of design professionals and to puzzle a home-seeking public.

The search for alternatives was not limited to one-off houses. From the outset, Australian architects kept in mind the house for everyman, just as an earlier generation of Australian architects such as Harold Desbrowe-Annear,

Walter Butler, Walter Burley Griffin and Marion Mahony had done in the first decades of the 20th Century, designing inexpensive cottage-like houses that might be available to all. A similar postwar quest found its peak in the mid-1960s with affordable architect-designed 'project houses', modest houses built by speculative builders that had architectural input to plan, form and finishes and were designed for the nuclear family in Australia's middle-class suburbs.[3] This was the antipodean parallel to the humanistic search in Europe for the ideal medium and high-density apartment type after the cataclysmic destruction of cities in World War II. Therein was (and largely still remains) the crucial difference between Australian cities and the urbanised centres of Europe and Asia. Dwelling is almost always associated with a detached house with space around it – the object in space – and virtually all Australian architectural histories, awards programs, and the cultural psyche of individual home ownership have fostered a concentration of physical and intellectual energy upon its design. In so doing, a rich history of apartment building since the early 20th Century has been neglected and the nuclear family has been stereotyped as the demographic model of Australian society.

Today in Australia, the journalistic brevity of Boyd's axiom still has relevance but needs lengthier and more detailed qualification. Even in the last ten years, much has changed. A new generation of young architects is now thinking differently, more critically, and in more modest and subtle terms. One of the most necessary qualifications is that the suburbs are no longer shunned. That shift occurred back in the mid-1970s, when Melbourne architects Edmond & Corrigan challenged the prevailing status quo of architectural good taste and suggested (in Venturi-style) that the ugly and

Poll House Dalkeith, Perth 2002
Architect: Gary Marinko

Australia: the reinterpretation of the 19th Century row house; the courtyard house type as an alternative to the suburban bungalow; and urban clusters of townhouses around shared designed landscapes. Now, single houses by architects such as Peter Tonkin and Ellen Woolley in Sydney, FIELD Consultants in Melbourne and Gary Marinko in Perth indicate that difficult questions are being asked of the house once again. Marinko's Poll House (2002), for example, is an introverted concrete courtyard house whose form to the street is a ghost of its hipped roof neighbours and a mute challenge to "the tumescent Tuscan villas of moneyed Perth".[5] In their mini-primer *Division and Multiplication*, young Melbourne architects Nigel Bertram and Kim Halik suggest the need to revisit the everyday of urban housing and its subdivision, and find in the familiar, lessons for the new.[6]

The social structure of architectural patronage in Australian domestic architecture has also changed. In the 1950s it was not uncommon for a young family to commission an architect to design a modest new home in a completely new suburban subdivision, or on a subdivided mansion estate, or in a difficult landscape site where no speculative builder dared go. In Australia today, it has to be said that this is a rare occurrence. Despite the nationally high standard of living and the persistent aspiration for single home-ownership, the financial ability to commission an architect-designed house has dissipated. This is partly because the culture of new suburban house building, which continued virtually unabated until the mid-1970s, has not only become difficult economically but also undesirable, given the unsustainable horizontal spread of Australian suburban sprawl. Today, new house blocks tend to be small, in the inner ring of suburbs close to urban amenities, and are burdened with accompanying labyrinthine planning controls and belligerently-defended heritage overlays.

Seven of the Australian houses featured in this book are located within situations rarely associated by international readers with the stereotypical images of Australian domestic architecture. These new houses are to be found in the older suburbs of late 18th and early 19th Century colonial townships with their planning basis in narrow-lot 19th Century speculative subdivision patterns, and with a non-

ordinary of Australian suburbia had virtue.[4] But the focus was primarily on institutional architecture and on questions of semiotics. The content of the suburbs – the houses and their prevailing subdivision patterns of quarter-acre blocks, common setbacks, side driveways and cameo front lawns – as an empirical laboratory for domestic architecture was not explored. Also overlooked were the numerous suggestions during the 1950s and 1960s for the alternative suburban house and the creation of an alternative reading of Australian urban morphology. During that time the hegemony of the garden suburb model was not uncritically accepted. Houses by Neil Clerehan, David Saunders and Graeme Gunn in Melbourne, Dickson & Platten in Adelaide, Don Gazzard, Michael Dysart and Ken Woolley in Sydney and John Railton in Brisbane suggested another future for urban dwelling in

Glick House Leederville, Perth 1999
Architect: Jane Wetherall and Geoff Warn

demonstrative materials palette of timber, brick and paint. These houses deal at a micro-level with different local urban morphologies and different climates. The three houses in Brisbane are tests, not just of dense living on small lots in a sub-tropical climate, but are conscientious searches for alternatives to the cottage version of the Queensland house, the traditionally preferred spreading bungalow in Australia's north. The two houses by Donovan Hill differ though, from that of Peter Skinner and Elizabeth Watson-Brown. Two slim lot houses that explore airiness and degrees of openness along their length are quite the opposite to the hollow-like site of the Skinner/Watson-Brown family house in leafy St.

Lucia, which uses a giant poinciana tree as its climatic and architectural foil to a giant glass wall facing the street.

Likewise in Perth, there are contrasting approaches taken within similar contexts. Warn & Wetherall's Glick House at Leederville suggests a low-tech bow to Modernist forebears, and a simultaneous nod to institutional aspirations with a fragile box-like form topped by a diaphanous cornice (which doubles as a roof terrace). Des Smith and Rosanna Blacket's house in Victoria Park is an expressionistic crafted folly hidden in an urban carpet of modest workers' housing, grafted onto the side wall of a garage. It is a house that might be a rustic cabin in a bush location, but appears magically at home in a landlocked block. In Sydney, Clinton Murray and Shelley Penn's 'Overcliffe' at Potts Point is another graft, this time onto the back of a small cottage and constructed of massive recycled timbers – a robust rural shed transplanted into the congested urbanity of Australia's most populous city. Thus each of these houses posits urban reform at the level of urban morphology, and each posits a future that is quietly contingent rather than heroic. In each, sustainability is an issue but never iconoclastic, a discussion that occurs at the level of urban consolidation and intelligently-made design choices – materials, orientation and structure. Each house is a deliberately blurred reflection, rather than a mirror of its context.

The only suburban house example is the Harbour House in Newcastle by Stutchbury & Pape (with Bourne Blue). Instead of reworking the suburban villa in this large industrial town north of Sydney, the form of the house was determined by its near neighbour, a 19th Century bishop's residence whose view had to be protected. The new house below is incised into the landscape, but with a parasol roof that creates a datum for a new villa type beneath, almost like an orangerie in the palace garden, a companion object in a much larger landscape, suggesting that the suburb itself might be considered not just for its urban qualities but also for the broader landscape that it might describe.

The other two Australian houses are landscape retreats. Fifty years ago, the simple inexpensive holiday house in timber and fibro-cement sheet was a realistic proposition for the average Australian family. Today, however, the newly commissioned retreat is still possible, but it is a rare privilege. For those clients who can afford it, the notion of apartment or townhouse living in the city can have a necessary outlet in the bush retreat, but more commonly in the beach house. Such retreats are not so much holiday houses as second houses, substantial alternatives to the city, and houses that encompass different evocations of dwelling. They are less formal, less materially precious, have looser notions of propriety, and above all, make a serious engagement with the coastal or rural landscape and the prospect of a vista.

The romance of Glenn Murcutt's corrugated-iron linear-planned houses in semi-rural bush landscapes[7] and Gabriel

'Overcliffe' Potts Point, Sydney, Australia 2002
Architect: Clinton Murray with Shelley Penn

Poole's canvas and steel pavilions in the rainforests of Queensland[8] characterised the international view of Australian architecture from the late 1970s to the mid-1990s. The two recent houses featured in this book suggest other responses to the house as a freestanding object within the Australian landscape. Their softness echoes not a singular reading of the landscape and how one might deal with it, but a sense that the Australian landscape might be negotiated in a myriad of ways, just as the local indigenous people had done before European settlement. They had marked their land in many ways, some to last forever, some to fade away with the weather, and some to maintain a dialogue, a conversation with the land.

On the windswept coast of Victoria, two options are proposed. On an open site outside Geelong, Kerstin

Thompson's House at Lake Connewarre resembles a meandering 'hide' that uses the contours of the land to mark itself across the landscape. The building's ordinariness in material and form is belied by this assured negotiation with the landscape. External spaces created by this house's meander are just as important as the prospect from its interior. By contrast, the Peninsula House by Sean Godsell is a battened box, monumental in its closed state and when seen in asymmetric aspect. Sun and shadow transform it to solid. But when its flaps are open, and sunlight strikes through its filigree, the house dissolves into that eternally captivating search in Australian architecture, the semi-enclosed outdoor space – the ideal place in which to dwell in this country – oscillating between permanence and the ephemeral delight of the dappled light of a tree branch overhead.

The small house in Australia remains the great testing ground of architectural experiment. It may be said that the skills and talents of these architects are wasted on private commissions in a society beset by the lack of a collective responsibility and acknowledgment of the public realm, but the individualist psyche of the average Australian has changed little in fifty years, and the endeavour of the small house continues to be a fruitful task. In Australia it has determined a culture, one initiated by a concerted reaction since colonial settlement to the 19th Century British aristocratic stranglehold on tenancy in relation to dwelling 'back Home'.[9] It has engendered a tradition of single-family detached houses that has resulted in a level of home-ownership envied by the rest of the world, though this level may be rapidly changing with increasing urban consolidation and rocketing real estate prices.

The collection of Australian houses illustrated in this book do not demonstrate a revolutionary future for the house, but offer careful critiques of the myths of Australian architecture and the ways in which Australians might live. They also offer critiques of the aggrandising ironies and too elegant simplicity of their elder colleagues in the profession. These are houses that indicate different architecture cultures[10] across the Australian continent, and yet common to each of them is a deliberate frugality in terms of materials, colour and structure, and also a conscientious, distilled and learned

knowledge of architecture that is not dependent on representation nor the allusions of historical type. This is not to say that these houses continue a hard line of progressivist abstraction. There are humbler principles at work, such as dealing with house-making in a brutally mercenary construction culture dependent on unskilled labour and off-the-shelf cladding techniques. The architects must also deal with the realities of the intelligent use of recycled materials, and they must gently engage with a landscape, neither in fear or loathing of it, nor in its triumphant conquest, but by celebrating its individuality and the fact that one might build within it or with it.

NOTES

1   Robin Boyd, preface to *Australia's Home*, Melbourne University Press, Melbourne, 1952.

2   Examples of houses designed by these architects and others can be found in Harry Seidler, *Houses, Interiors and Projects*, Associated General Publishers, Sydney 1954 ; Neil Clerehan, *Best Australian Houses*, Cheshire, Melbourne, 1961; Michael Markham and Meghan Nordeck, *Geoffrey Summerhayes: architectural projects*, School of Architecture, University of Western Australia, Nedlands, 1993;and Robin Boyd, *Living in Australia*, Pergamon Press, Sydney 1970.

3   The best known examples of 1960s project houses in Australia were those designed by architects Ken Woolley and Michael Dysart and sold by Pettit and Sevitt in Sydney (1964–65), and those designed by Graeme Gunn for Merchant Builders in Melbourne (1965).

4   Conrad Hamann, *Cities of hope : Australian architecture and design by Edmond and Corrigan*, 1962–1992, Oxford University Press, Melbourne, 1993.

5   Nigel Westbrook, "A landscape of objects", *Architecture Australia*, vol.91, no.5, September/October 2002, pp56-61.

6   Nigel Bertram and Kim Halik, *Division and Multiplication*, RMIT University Press, Melbourne, 2002.

7   E. M. Farrelly, *Three houses, Glenn Murcutt*, Phaidon, London 1993; Haig Beck and Jackie Cooper (eds.), *Glenn Murcutt: A singular architecture practice*, Images Publishing Group, Mulgrave, Victoria 2001; and Francois Fromonot, *Glenn Murcutt: works and projects*, 1969–2001, Thames & Hudson, London 2003.

8   Bruce Walker, *Gabriel Poole: space in which the soul can play*, Visionary Press, Noosa, Queensland 1998.

9   Alistair Greig, *The stuff dreams are made of: Housing Provision in Australia*, 1945–1960, Melbourne University Press, Melbourne 1995; Patrick Troy (ed.), *A History of European Housing in Australia*, Cambridge University Press, Melbourne, 2000.

10 Philip Goad, *New Directions in Australian Architecture*, Pesaro Publishing, Balmain, NSW 2001.

Peninsula House Mornington Peninsula, Australia 2002 >
Architect: Sean Godsell

MAKING A DIFFERENCE: NEW ZEALAND HOUSES AT THE BEGINNING OF THE 21ST CENTURY

BY JUSTINE CLARK AND PAUL WALKER

Justine Clark has a BArch (hons) from the University of Auckland and a MArch (dist) from Victoria University of Wellington. She is editor of Architecture Australia. Paul Walker has a BArch (hons) and a PhD from the University of Auckland. He is Associate Professor of Architecture at the University of Melbourne.

THE HISTORICAL CONTEXT

At the beginning of the New Zealand film 'Once Were Warriors', the camera pulls back from a green pastoral scene to reveal that this is an image on an advertising hoarding in a bleak South Auckland urban setting.¹ It's a moment of shock for those who believe the cliché of New Zealand's green image. They can take comfort from the unconvincing end of the film, however, when the landscape is once again asserted to be the antidote to the inauthentic and destructive world of the city.

Whether or not its finale persuades, 'Once Were Warriors' graphically points to contradictions in New Zealand's cultural identity. It is one of the most highly urbanised nations in the world, but continues to define and promote itself according to rural images of peaceful pastures and beautiful dramatic landscapes. New Zealand belongs to the world's privileged group of developed nations and understands itself as part of the West, but its cultural vibrancy – in popular music, the fine arts, literature and film – increasingly comes from Maori and from Pacific Island and Asian communities.

New Zealand's architecture is only beginning to come to terms with the country's non-Western heritage, but it is deeply affected by the preoccupation with landscape. This preoccupation reflects the country's history and its current economic reliance on exporting farm and horticultural commodities, and on attracting tourists to gaze at the scenery. It also reflects how the country's image is partially shaped by external expectations that this is what the place should be.

New Zealand is a small South Pacific country, an archipelago with a land mass of similar size to that of the British Isles or Japan, with dramatically varied topography and a mild maritime climate. 75 percent of the population of 4 million are the descendents of European settlers who began arriving after 1840. That year, the Treaty of Waitangi was signed: principal Maori chiefs recognized the authority of the British Crown in exchange for protection of traditional rights and customs. The Treaty did not stop Maori losing most of their lands, particularly those suited to agriculture, in violent confrontations with settlers in the following decades. Today Maori constitute 15 percent of the nation's inhabitants; Asian and Pacific Islander migrants make up other significant minorities.

New Zealand cities are relatively small in population, but they do spread over vast suburban territories. The largest is Auckland, a fast growing metropolitan area with 1.2 million people. The next in size are Wellington, the capital, and Christchurch, each with about 350,000. Their character comes from their sprawl and from the dominant suburban building type: the freestanding single family house. By the end of the 19th Century, New Zealand popular housing was derived from American models: local wooden 'bay villas' of the 1880s & 90s are similar to San Francisco houses of the 1870s. The California bungalow that emerged in Los Angeles at the beginning of the 20th Century was the dominant house type in New Zealand by the 1920s.² Architecturally designed houses, by contrast, continued to be heavily influenced by British precedents, though some architects who worked in this manner (Samuel Hurst Seager, Frederick de Jersey Clere and William Gray Young) suggested that New Zealand architecture needed to respond to climate, materials and the local way of life.

By the mid 20th Century things had changed. In response to the housing crisis caused by the 1930s economic depression, New Zealand's first Labour Party government from 1937 built tens of thousands of 'state houses'. Conservative in layout and look, and modelled by the architects on English cottages, they were a unique development that influenced the country's housing market even after it was returned to private enterprise and American good-life fantasies in the 1950s.

By then, new housing models – Modernist ones – were also available. European Modernism had been discussed in New Zealand since the 1920s, but the Modernism that emerged in practice was different. In 1946 a group of architectural students in Auckland who called themselves the 'Architectural Group' published a manifesto, 'On the Necessity for Architecture', which attacked poorly planned suburbs and promoted a Modern architecture based on standardization and machine production. It also called for a particularly New Zealand architecture: "New Zealand must have its own architecture, its own sense of what is beautiful and appropriate to our climate and conditions."[3] The Modernism that the 'Group' wanted was not the International Style, but the regionally inflected mode that had emerged in many disparate locations around the world at this time. What this meant in practical terms for the members of the 'Group' became apparent when they started building houses in 1950: long low-pitched roofs, exposed timber used both as structure and cladding in technically inventive and economic ways, and open planning with wide glass doors to connect interior and exterior. The sites they built on were outer suburban ones, oblivious to the city proper.

Precedents for this kind of work could have been found in domestic work in California and Scandinavia. But in the years after the New Zealand 'Centennial' in 1940 local architects also claimed local precedents in the simple farm buildings and houses of the earliest period of European presence in New Zealand. These were embraced while early grander institutional buildings were reviled for their pretentiousness. Old colonial houses were reputed to have a relationship with the 'natural' conditions of climate, site and materials. Mid 19th Century British settlers were refigured as 'pioneers' in a developing New Zealand architectural

discourse in the 1940s and 50s that implicitly linked a functionalist local heritage with the 'pioneers' described in international discussion of Modern architecture, notably in Nikolaus Pevsner's 1936 book *Pioneers of the Modern Movement*.[4]

House forms in New Zealand are not radically different from those in many other places, but by the middle of the 20th Century the idea of the house had a peculiarly powerful role in the New Zealand imagination. This came from the economic and emotional importance of the house: it was the only kind of habitation most people knew and the largest single economic investment they were ever likely to make. This perception was exacerbated during the years after World War II when, despite the state housing program, there were major housing shortages. Local historical precedents licensed a conflation of New Zealand's colonial pragmatism with Modern functionalism, and New Zealand architecture became identified with the small, locally-inflected Modern house. As New Zealand architecture came to be known better in the international media in the 1950s, it was on the house that European publications settled to represent New Zealand architecture to the world. It is in these terms that New Zealand architecture continues to be understood.

THE HOUSE AS A SITE OF INQUIRY

The cost of privileging the house in architectural discourse has been the neglect of the urban realm, including the suburbia attendant on the house's proliferation. Although the view that New Zealand architecture is the house in a setting of natural or at least rural landscape (the ideal to which the suburban house aspires) is widely accepted and is still promoted today, there were alternative views. But they did not gain any wide circulation. The Wellington equivalent of Auckland's 'Group', the 'Architectural Centre', has fought for decades to improve urban conditions, consistently opposing the sprawl of dispersed single family houses.

While there are problems in the focus on the single house, this focus also creates opportunities. Understood by architects internationally during the 20th Century as the site of experiment, houses have been where ideas have been tested and positions expressed in a contained manner, which has then informed larger scale and more public work. But this view too lightly puts aside the very conservatism of the house which is, after all, the scene of the nuclear family's social reproduction, and a setting for reinforcing conventional modes of sociality. It also disregards problems involved in translating what the architect might learn from domestic design into different building types and scales.

It is also interesting to consider the way houses can connect directly with the larger scale, the collective: city, suburb, community, polity. Not houses as trial runs for other types of architecture, but as buildings that can have a direct effect. After all, the private and public are not distinct worlds – the civic is always already invested in the domestic and vice versa. Houses that explore this connectivity, and that offer some kind of provocation to both architecture and the broader culture, have the potential to make a difference. They have a quality that might be called 'difficult', suggesting a kind of disruptive agency, exceeding the comfortable pigeon-hole of 'experiment'. A 'difficult' house might construct reference within itself to the wider conditions in which it is situated. But to have consequence, a 'difficult' house needs to assert something to those who see it. This could be so through publication, a very important strategy in 20th Century architecture. Or it might pull its physical location into focus, asking us to take a second look at the suburb, city or rural environment in which it sits. Such houses project themselves within their physical contexts, but insist on being seen not merely for us to admire them – in the manner of the trophy house – but to make us think.

The disruptive look of the 'difficult' house might be overt. The most blatant New Zealand example is architect Rewi Thompson's own house in Auckland's eastern suburbs (1985). The Thompson house is a plywood ziggurat, aggressive in its form and its apparent facelessness – no windows or doors are visible in its street front. It stands close to the street edge in contrast to its neighbours which politely recede behind lawns and gardens.⁵ Its closest rival in this mode of confrontation is Ian Athfield's house-as-anti-suburban-manifesto of a generation earlier. Poised above the harbourside motorway in Wellington, it is constructed as a

Park Mews Hataitai, Wellington 1974
Architect: Roger Walker

Athfield House Khandallah, Wellington 1966–
Architect: Ian Athfield

Rewi Thompson House Kohimarama, Auckland 1985
Architect: Rewi Thompson

village-like mix of colonial, vernacular and High Modern references. This house physically confronts the suburb from within its midst. It proffers an immediate other to the surroundings. With the contemporaneous work of Roger Walker, it initiated a new approach to housing in New Zealand in the late 1960s.

However, unlike the directness of the Thompson and Athfield houses, most New Zealand architects demonstrate their attitude to suburbia by turning away from it. The conventional alternative to the suburb is to project the

context of the house as being landscape – more or less natural landscape. But there is no 'natural' landscape per se – it is always shaped or interpreted. A 'difficult' house will make this explicit. Here pervasive differences between Australian and New Zealand responses can be identified. Both countries have examples of diverse approaches, but in general the Australian architect's wish is to hover over the land, the New Zealander's to shape it. Land in New Zealand is understood as already shaped – by earthquake, volcano, and by the human hand that has carved the terraced sites of

Waitamariki House Northland 1998
Architect: Mitchell and Stout

pa (Maori fortified settlements), cleared farmland and constructed the massive hydro-electric dams.[6] And there is always a sense that the land might, quite suddenly, move again.

Of the projects in this book, Mitchell Stout's Waitamairiki House reshapes its site most overtly. The building carves into the hill, the earth dramatically piled back on top. Nearby at the Rawhiti House by Fearon Hay the intervention is less dramatic, but here too the hill is cut to make terraces for a sheltered courtyard behind the assemblage of buildings. Even in the urban Oriental Bay House in Wellington, the sense of house as a reconfiguration of the ground is apparent. These

gestures are not innocent ones even if few will see them: they assert a form of negotiation with the landscape.

If the turn to the landscape is a longstanding tradition in New Zealand domestic architecture, the turn to the city is relatively new. Recent writing on the effects of information technology warns of the dissolution of the city, proposing that hospitals will be replaced by telemedicine, museums and libraries by databases, shops by e-commerce, prisons by electronic surveillance, and so on.[7] This view argues that urban intensity will be dispersed, as we no longer need face to face encounters to get things done. But what is striking

Wakefield Street Apartments Wellington 2000
Architect: Architecture Workshop (James Fenton)

about the urban centres of New Zealand's cities (like those in many countries) is that they have been reinvigorated or at least gentrified, with new institutional and commercial buildings and with new populations of visitors and residents. People apparently want to be in town as much as they want to be at the beach or in the mountains. The city has become a new fantasy, strongly fed by images of stylish urban accommodations published in international magazines such as *Wallpaper**. Some of the resulting domestic architecture has sought retreat in the urban environment, as much as retreat might be sought at an isolated beach or forest site,

unlike the two New Zealand urban houses in this book. The Wakefield St Apartments and the Oriental Bay House perch on precipitous sites, highly visible within the city of Wellington. They relate to the city by placing themselves overtly within it: they take cityscape as landscape to see and be seen from. Both blur conventional expectations of what domestic architecture should look like and where it should be located. They blur differences between public and private, home and commerce, to suggest new models of both while also addressing the questions raised about the future of the inner city by the 'Architectural Centre' some 50 years ago.

Rawhiti House Northland 1999
Architect: Fearon Hay

SUBURBIA AND CULTURAL DIFFERENCE

The issue of suburbia remains. New Zealand has no architect-champion for its suburbs, no equivalent of the American Robert Venturi or Australian Peter Corrigan. 'Difficult' houses have not yet faced the difficulty of seeing the suburb as a positive. But there are architects who take suburbia seriously; and for many sole practitioners without the profile of 'star' designers, a practice based in house alterations may be a strong social commitment as well as a means to make a living. Nevertheless, New Zealand architecture overlooks the suburb, the collective outcome of

the building type which it privileges, the single-family house.

This is because domesticity itself, the messiness of ordinary life, is a challenge for architecture. The everyday social program of the house is not an unchanging static thing, but a constantly shifting field of activity. Different people live in houses in different ways. They make their own interventions and accommodate themselves in their houses by filling them with the accoutrements of their daily lives, or through do-it-yourself interventions as a way of making a place in the world – of creating 'home'. These things represent a difficulty to architecture by disturbing its formalist presumptions. It is a difficulty that has been articulated most clearly by feminist writing on domesticity.[8] If houses are to make a difference to architecture and culture, architecture needs to engage with these 'untidy' worlds where society is built.

The emergent multi-culturalism of New Zealand cities makes such rethinking of the house a priority. Alongside embracing landscape as a cultural construct and rethinking the relationship of the domestic environment to the city, this is the principal challenge facing the house at the beginning of the 21st Century.

In the suburbs of Auckland, architects Gordon Moller, Patrick Clifford and Marshall Cook are examining how standard 'state house' plans, devised for standard New Zealand families, might best be changed to accommodate families of various sizes, structures, modes of inhabitation and cultural backgrounds.[9] This formally modest but socially important work is being undertaken for the government agency Housing New Zealand, responsible for helping those without the resources to enter the private housing market. There may no longer be the accommodation shortages that focused the concerns of post-war architects on the single family house, but poor quality and inappropriately planned houses remain a problem.

Multi-culturalism also has an up-market aspect. The image of the free-standing suburban house typical of New World cities and the lifestyle that goes with it is a fantasy drawing Asian migration to burgeoning Auckland (as well as Perth, Sydney, Vancouver, Toronto etc). This suburban fantasy is the converse of the fantasy of urban life and the apartment that has taken hold of the educated middle class's imagination. It does not leave the suburb unchanged. This can be seen in those outer eastern suburbs of Auckland favoured by middle class families who have moved from Hong Kong and Taipei. They have controversially inflected the New Zealand suburban house according to different images of amenity and desirability. For example, these houses consistently monumentalise the front entry, assertively using ersatz classical elements to a rare degree, and they appear over-scaled on their tight lots.

There has been a tendency within architectural criticism to understand work outside the metropolitan centres of America and Europe in terms of a trickle of influence from those centres, or as a regionalist inflection of the international norm.[10] The issue of how architecture is made in our part of the world inevitably returns to these models. But Asia and the Pacific have long been places of mutual interaction and exchange, and of what architectural writer Stephen Cairns calls "trans-local affiliations". This does not entail the one-way export of architecture from nominal centre to regional periphery. Rather it suggests networks of exchange and speculation. The architects and critics of the 21st Century will reinvigorate this idea of exchange and use it to re-examine the architectural production of each place and culture. This is a key issue for New Zealand as the country's sense of itself as part of the Pacific is more and more deeply felt. It is also the country's greatest opportunity.

NOTES

1   Once Were Warriors, 1994, Lee Tamahori director

2   See William Toomath, *Built in New Zealand: The Houses We Live In*, Auckland: HarperCollins, 1996

3   See Justine Clark & Paul Walker, *Looking for the Local: Architecture and the New Zealand Modern*, Wellington: Victoria University Press, 2000: p30

4   Clark & Walker, p29

5   Ross Jenner, 'The Experience of Rewi Thompson: A Crossroads in New Zealand', *Lotus* no 105 (June 2000) p 119

6   This notion is suggested, for example, in the very title of Barry Brailsford's book on archaeology of Maori site, *The Tattooed Land*, 2nd ed Hamilton, NZ: Stoneprint Press 1997.

7   See for example William Mitchell, *City of Bits*, Cambridge, Ma.: MIT Press, 1995, chapter 2 'Recombinant Architecture'

8   See for example: Sarah Treadwell, 'From the Margins of Architecture: An Account of Domestic Chaos', unpublished lecture, 1989; Paula E Geyh, 'Burning Down the House? Domestic Space and Feminine Subjectivity in Marilynne Robinson's *Housekeeping*', *Contemporary Literature*, vol 34 no 1, 1993: 103–122; Jennifer Bloomer, 'Nature Morte', in Francesca Hughes, ed, *The Architect: Reconstructing Her Practice*, Cambridge, Ma: MIT Press, 1996: 237–250; Joanne Besley 'Home Improvement, the popular and the everyday', in In the Making: Architecture's Past, proceedings of the 18th annual conference of the Society of Architectural Historians, Australia and New Zealand, Darwin: SAHANZ, 2001: 305–312.

9   See 'No-frills house draws high-profile architect', *The New Zealand Herald*, 5 May 2001.

10 On regionalism, see Kenneth Frampton, 'Towards a Critical Regionalism', in Hal Foster, ed, *The Anti-Aesthetic*, Port Townsend, Washington: Bay Press, 1983; Alexander Tzonis & Liane Lefaivre, 'Critical Regionalism' in Michael Speaks, ed, *The Critical Landscape*, Rotterdam: 010 Publishers, 1996.

A CONCISE HISTORY OF FUTURE HOUSES –
ON THE 'OTHER' SIDE OF THE WORLD

BY PHILIP GOAD

Philip Goad is Professor of Architecture and Deputy Dean of the Faculty of Architecture, Building and Planning at The University of Melbourne.

A critical project of Modernism in 20th Century architecture has been the house. It has been the ideal laboratory, not only for new form but also new ways of living, and for testing new propositions about how one might dwell in a future world, and in a future city. During the 1920s, Le Corbusier was the prima donna prophet for the future house. Whether an expensive villa for a Parisian industrialist, a demonstration pavilion, or small weekender, each house was a deliberate polemical statement for reform. Each house was an argument for anti-orthodoxy, and each followed, according to Le Corbusier's artistic agenda, a carefully orchestrated path of aesthetic experiment. It must be noted that not all of these houses were successes, nor did they inevitable result in the progeny so confidently forecast by their designer. Each house was hardly a true *machine a habiter* (machine for living in), one of his major claims. Almost all of Le Corbusier's 'white' villas, the projected exemplars of industrial production, had walls of painted cement render over terra cotta block-work. His Petite Maison de Weekend (Villa Felix), built in 1935, employed industrial Nevada glass tiles, plywood lining, and apparently mass-produced factory-shed concrete vaults, yet its plan consisted of a group of cell-like clusters half-buried into the landscape with sod roofs overhead.[1] This "back to earth living unit for a modern businessman" was embedded in romantic idealism.

Le Corbusier was not alone. A common cause amongst the early architectural Modernist was the search for an appropriate dwelling for everyman. It was a shared ethical goal that linked serious rationalists such as Ludwig Hilbersheimer to technocrats like Buckminster Fuller. The everyday materials and domestic forms of Heinrich Tessenow were linked to the *sachlich* forms of JJP Oud,

Hans Schmidt and Wassily Luckhardt, and even the works of an idiosyncratic individualist like Rudolph Schindler. The reinforced concrete and timber Pueblo Ribera apartments by Schindler, La Jolla, California (1923-25) can still be regarded as powerful exemplars of courtyard housing and rational construction.

After World War II, the vision of the future house shifted. The cataclysmic events of war now lent a cynical edge to polemics of the future. As Esther McCoy shrewdly observed, the postwar house seemed to embody "a marriage between Walden Pond and Douglas Aircraft".[3] This fusion between romantic nature and technology can be recognised even in Mies van der Rohe's famous house for Dr Edith Farnsworth at Plano, Illinois (1945-50) – a steel and glass diagram of Semper's four elements of architecture complete with Chinese shantung curtains. This proposition for a simplified existence embodied an archaic simplicity that was fundamentally anti-urban and individualistic. Its polemic was strong, too strong, and the client sued the architect in ignominious circumstances, but the Farnsworth House was destined to become notorious as a glimpse of a possible future. As an ideal it had immediate influence, from the work of Philip Johnson and Craig Ellwood in the 1950s and 1960s to Glenn Murcutt's recent elegant domestic sheds in Australia. One house had thus engendered multiple interpretations.

At the same time, a younger postwar generation reacted with completely different house propositions. In some cases these were houses that suggested no exteriority, only interiority. One was a courtyard house that implied an amoebic cave – Peter and Alison Smithson's 'House of the Future',

Pueblo Ribera Apartments La Jolla, California, USA 1923–25
Architect: Rudolph Schindler

designed for the *Daily Mail* Ideal Homes Exhibition, London (1956). This was a proposal that was urban, implied density and had no greater landscape than its immediate private centre. The 'House of the Future' was a fusion of

Le Corbusier's Citrohan/Citroen (a house built like a motor car) and one of the most traditional types of architectural conceptions, the patio-dwelling. A simple box without external windows and a door on only one side, with rooms placed freely around a patio, like compartments of a cave. Each compartment was a different size, a different area, and a different height – a totally differentiated shape to achieve its purpose.[4]

But on the 'other' side of the world, the house of the future cannot be traced to such easily identifiable didactic oppositions. If any detached house type had dominated South and Southeast Asia, South America, Central and South Africa, Australia and New Zealand by the 1920s (through complete hybrid technologies and complex cultural transfer) it was the bungalow. As a house type, there was no better. It was adaptable, regionally appropriate, lightweight in construction and climatically sensitive. It was, as Anthony King has observed, the perfect global type.[5] While the European avant-garde had developed its own polemical types, on the 'other' side of the world the idea of the future house was induced from a different reaction. Architects, imbued with the idea of modernist reform, reacted to the popular success of the bungalow type, its colonial associations, its appearance and its construction. Acting as a spur to this was the exponential growth and embrace of Western construction practices, especially the replacement of traditional building materials, such as timber, with the technology of reinforced concrete. In addition to this, due to differences in scale, economy, and climatic determinants, the role of the detached house in many parts of the region became involved with politics, and equity, and asked questions of fundamental need.

Within the region there were extraordinary contrasts. The middle class suburbs of Australia and New Zealand were a far cry from the urban chaos of Calcutta, or indeed a fledgling Singapore reconstructing itself after the war. Yet despite these differences, and the incredibly diverse ranges of negotiation and agency, architects working on this 'other' side of the world have tended to follow three paths in thinking about the future house: 1) the single house as a modernist project that continues to tackle – but critically – the New World city's specificity of climate and colonial planning;

2) the use of alternative labour technologies as a response to the immediate circumstances of practice and issues of local political economy; and 3) the complete retreat from the city, the house as 'low-tech', small, and 'anti-bungalow' and reformist rather than nostalgic in aesthetic.

REFORMING THE CITY

In the 1964 book, *Tropical Architecture in the Dry and Humid Zones*, Maxwell Fry and Jane Drew defined the tropics as a specific geographic band determined by that part of the world either side of the equator with two distinctive climates of the hot-dry and the humid tropics.[6] This was a typically scientific and simplistic approach to the functional determinant of climate. Overlooked were the cultural history and building traditions of the region under examination. But Fry and Drew had opened the possibility for looking at reform primarily through the focus of climate determining the house form. It became the rationale for localising the universal tendencies of pre-war Modernism without jettisoning its functionalist ethos. The result was a hybrid Modernism, neither pure nor with regional alliteration, but as the natural outgrowth of 'acclimatization'. The clearest

evidence of testing their proposition was in the row housing (1956–) of Chandigarh, the new capital of the north Indian state of Punjab. The result was a series of inventively planned houses where cross-ventilation, breeze-block walls and rationalised planning offered economies of scale and the promise of hygiene and open space, models that have seen further application in cities from Capetown to Jakarta.

In Brazil, such experiments were tried earlier, and were eminently successful. Oscar Niemeyer's house design for Henrique Xavier in Rio de Janeiro (1936) was a considered critique of Le Corbusier's five points of architecture. It was an aerated urban town house designed over four levels, each level unrelated to the other, and described by Stamo Papadaki as a "dwelling tree".[7] By 1952, at the Parque Guinle residential complex in Rio de Janeiro, Lucio Costa had transformed such experiments into models for future apartments with completely screened walls that indicated new formal possibilities for the New World city. Affonso Reidy's Pedregulho housing in Rio de Janeiro (1955) took such ideals even further, creating an entire urban precinct from a snaking linear apartment block. In the United States, the married student housing at New Haven, Connecticut (1960-61) by Paul Rudolph, a complex of brick and concrete apartments that resembled an Italian hill-town, would find its ultimate realisation in the Colonnade Apartments in Singapore (1979-87). In Australia, Robin Boyd's house in Melbourne's South Yarra (1957) reinterpreted the local 19th Century colonial terrace house with a sliver-like courtyard house covered by a draped catenary roof.[8] More recently in another Melbourne project, in the Holyoake House, Hawthorn (2000) FIELD Consultants realised a further complex hybrid: transforming the 19th Century Australian worker's cottage with a nod not just to the ethos of the Arts and Architecture Case Study House program but also to the formal models firmly based in Australian house experiments of the 1950s.[9] In each of these apartment and single house designs, the results are productive hybrids at once critical of and supportive of the Modernist project, yet located firmly within the question of dwelling in a postcolonial city.

Xavier House Rio de Janeiro, Brazil 1936
Architect: Oscar Niemeyer

Colonnade Apartments Singapore 1979–87 >
Architect: Paul Rudolph

REFORMING PRACTICE

The second path for the future house on the 'other' side of the world has been the use of alternative labour technologies as a response to the immediate circumstances of practice and issues of political economy. In 1949, Charles Eames used black-painted standard Crittalls window sections to define a free and open matrix for his own house in Pacific Palisades, a house with infills of clear and obscure glass, and gold, red, black and blue panels. Eames and his wife Ray furnished the house with vernacular *objets' d'arts* collected on their travels and exquisitely engineered furniture of their own design. Theirs was a freedom of expression that would have prophetic consequences. The Eames House would be revolutionary in its possibilities for a no rules architecture that was still rational at the core of its inception.

On the 'other' side of the world, such elegant artlessness would find few parallels. In many other cultures, a similar ethic and desire for freedom in providing a simple backdrop for living was founded on a completely different form of practice, one based on the exigencies of local constructional practices and modest economies. Amancio Guedes in Mozambique, Hassan Fathy in Egypt, Johan Silas in Indonesia, and Laurie Baker in India would all base their careers on the material and infrastructural limits of their local cultures. The humility of their practices had parallels to the Eames' wish to dismantle aesthetic pretension, but these architects had challenges infinitely more complex. They were building in developing countries, acting as designers, and interloping in a cultural milieu (even if it were their own) where the designer traditionally had no part, and attempting in some way to ameliorate, and expedite, the process of providing home. While architects in Europe and the United States, such as Aldo Van Eyck and Bernard Rudofsky, would pinpoint and highlight forgotten links between anthropology and architecture and suggest the need for an existential return to the roots of architecture,[10] these other architects were actually building. Baker, for example, in exploring the brick *jalis* (perforated screens), traditional roofs, stepped arches and the spatial limits of local masonry construction, designed a series of houses that would be described as "revolutionary in its simplicity". Baker's approach is disarmingly and provocatively ingenuous:

"I learn my architecture by watching what ordinary people do; in any case it is always the cheapest and simplest because ordinary people do it."[11]

It is a statement that has the quality of a timeless proverb, made more potent by the yawning gap between those who 'have' and those who 'have not' in a non-Western building environment, but also because he and likeminded architects create different 'future houses', not behind in physical time, but simply different. Such houses suggest that the term 'future' must always be negotiated with the phenomenological realities of time and place.

REFORMING THE RETREAT

The third path for the future house on the 'other' side of the world has been the complete retreat from the city. Romantic in spirit, this has not meant the large country estate but the small hut, the cabin in the wilderness. Diminutive size has contributed a necessary humility in the face of an invariably larger and omniscient landscape. In Europe, such a tradition is understood by the dachas of Latvia and Estonia on the Baltic, the summerhouses of Swedish islands or in a house such as Alvar Aalto's experimental summer retreat at Muuratsalo Finland (1953). In the United States, such examples as Frank Lloyd Wright's Ocatilla Desert Camp, Chandler, Arizona (1929) and Rudolph & Twitchell's 1950s houses with their adjustable flaps and parasol roofs in Sarasota, Florida, celebrated a deliberate low-tech approach to creating architecture and defining the spaces of living, almost one of making do, but in that making, discovering. In New Zealand, this habit is found in the tradition of the 'bach', constructing home-built seaside cottages, often from second-hand materials and on difficult sites.[12] In Australia, this does not mean the sophisticated Miesian musings of Glenn Murcutt's linear houses in rural and bush locations, but either the pragmatically constructed tree house, or the pavilion in the bush. Bill and Ruth Lucas's own house (1957) perched across a Castlecrag gully is Sydney's tribute to the Swiss family Robinson, but constructed with Heath Robinson-like ingenuity. It is a house of Georgian-wired glass, exposed aluminium foil insulation, and steel frame and wire struts. Roy Grounds' retreat (1965) at Bithry Inlet on the south coast of New South Wales was a sod-roofed tee-pee constructed of plantation-grown indigenous timbers. With open sides and roll-down canvas blinds, it was the perfect permanent tent.[13]

Each of these houses invokes a tense dialogue between an invented existence without historical reference, and a landscape that demands survival within it. There is a rusticity that suggests the inclusion of the hand, but not a nostalgic return to the reactionary whim of the Arts and Crafts. These houses bear the mark of a newly intelligent and self-aware craftsman, rather like the visionary boat-builder – the maker of an object which must deal with nature's most fundamental elements: wind, light and rain. Such houses forecast an alternative future in which landscape and its sustainability can render the architecture subservient to the landscape's physical necessity. In other words, the house becomes a staging point for living in and experiencing the landscape, a staging point that is not outdated and unfashionable but increasingly the measure and the goal of a desired future. On the 'other' side of the world, such a future is still possible to realise.

TODAY'S FUTURE HOUSES

In each case of these three directions for reform, the rationale was place-centred and existential. The future was not confidently portrayed, but negotiated. Unlike the dreamy villas and hotels of Sri Lankan architect Geoffrey Bawa, whose works bespeak a peaceful reconciliation between colonial and contemporary Sri Lanka, or the gracious Georgian-Modern houses of Australian architect Guilford Bell, future houses of the region suggest grittier realities.

The houses in this book follow these three generalised paths of reform. They are not easy essays in so-called regionalism, and in many cases their budgets are not small. Yet, they point to different realities where the detached house still has relevance to inform a discussion on ways of living. An interesting aspect to this collection is that all (apart from Thailand) are located in postcolonial countries where the debates on urbanism fluctuate rapidly. The fate of the future city in this region is undecided, its history is not yet written.

Construction practices fluctuate between sophistication and archaism, and the question of landscape continues to play an intrinsic role, i.e. the dialogue is a new one, and climate still has the power to dictate specific formal decisions. The project of the detached house remains a modern quest, but it has become a continuing and relevant experiment for the 21st Century on this 'other' side of the world.

NOTES

1 Le Corbusier and Pierre Jeanneret, *Oeuvre complete 1934–1938*, Les Editions d'Architecture, Zurich, 1964, pp124–130.

2 Tim Benton, "Six Houses", in *Le Corbusier: Architect of the Century*, Arts Council of Great Britain, London, 1987, pp65–66.

3 Esther McCoy, "West Coast Architects V: John Lautner", *Arts and Architecture*, August 1965, p22.

4 "House of the Future at the Ideal Homes Exhibition", *Architectural Design*, March 1956, pp101–102; Reyner Banham, *The New Brutalism: Ethic or Aesthetic?*, The Architectural Press, London, 1966, pp62–64; *Alison and Peter Smithson – The Shift*, Architectural Monographs, Academy Editions, London, 1982, pp44–46, 80–85.

5 Anthony D. King, *The Bungalow: The production of a global culture*, Routledge & Kegan Paul, London, 1984.

6 Maxwell Fry and Jane Drew, *Tropical Architecture in the dry and humid zones*, Batsford, London, 1964. This was an updated version of their earlier *Tropical Architecture in the humid zone*, Batsford, London, 1956, pp27, 34–39.

7 Papadaki borrows the term dwelling tree from Gaston Bachelard's *L'Air et les Songes*, Jose Corti, Paris, 1943. See Stamo Papadaki, *Oscar Niemeyer*, George Braziller, New York, 1960, p13.

8 "House in South Yarra, Victoria", *Architecture in Australia*, vol.49, no.1, March 1960, pp86–93; *The Architectural Review*, vol.128, no.765, November 1960, pp332–335; JM Richards, *New Buildings in the Commonwealth*, The Architectural Press, London 1961, pp36–37.

9 Rewi Thompson, "Field Day", *Architectural Review Australia*, 73, Spring 2000, pp38–45.

10 See Francis Strauven, *Aldo van Eyck: the shape of relativity*, Architectura & Natura, Amsterdam, 1998 and Felicity Scott, "Bernard Rudofsky: Allegories of Nomadism and Dwelling", in Sarah Williams Goldhagen and Réjean Legault (eds.), *Anxious Modernisms: experimentation in postwar architectural culture*, MIT Press, Cambridge, Mass., 2000, pp215–237.

11 Laurie Baker, quoted in Gautam Bhatia, *Laurie Baker: life, work and writings*, Penguin, New Delhi (1991), 1994, p3.

12 Peter Wood, "The Bach: The Cultural History of a Local Typology", *Fabrications*, vol.11, no.1, July 2000, pp44–61.

13 Philip Goad, "Locating Dymaxion: International Myth, Local Reality", in Michael J Ostwald and R John Moore (eds.), *Re-framing architecture: theory, science and myth*, Archadia Press, Sydney, 2000, pp79–85.

KARN BOONTARIK

Lubid Studio Bangkok, Thailand 2003

Karn Boontarik worked for six years in the field of art and industrial design in the USA, before returning to his hometown of Bangkok to open the Lubid Studio. He claims this studio to be influenced by the liberalism of San Francisco. It may also reflect the eclecticism of Bangkok and the ongoing American cultural influence on Bangkok. The building takes great inspiration from the Case Study House – No 8 (1949) by Charles and Ray Eames in Pacific Palisades, which was also a combination of house and studio.

The Lubid Studio required a number of spaces for living, working and outdoor relaxation. The double-height workshop occupies the central space in the building, with bright red doors and yellow wall panels. The internal stairs are constructed from railway timber, and lead up to offices on the first floor and double-height living quarters on the second floor. Natural light and ventilation permeates the building at every opportunity, and Karn has coated the rough concrete surfaces with Urethane. The structure remains

internal work space

east elevation >

exposed and bright colours are utilized, giving the building an honest industrialized appearance.

A rough timber deck sits on the street in front of the house, and this is a stage for a constantly changing display of artefacts. The Lubid Studio becomes a venue for community engagement and interaction. The courtyard swimming pool with sexy sculptures reveals Karn's fascination with American paraphernalia and the Coca-Cola aesthetic.

PIRAK ANURAKYAWACHON

east elevation

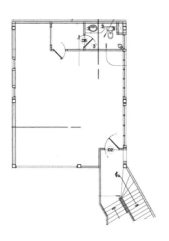

ground floor plan

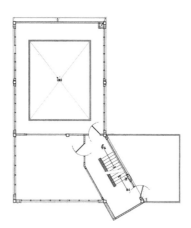

1st floor plan

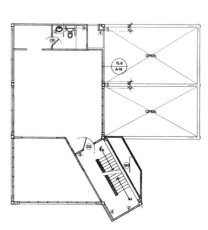

2nd floor plan

Lubid Studio Bangkok, Thailand 2003

view of courtyard from west

STUTCHBURY AND PAPE
WITH BOURNE BLUE

Harbour House Cooks Hill, Newcastle, NSW, Australia 2003

ground floor

< north elevation

The theme of the roof as floating parasol has informed houses and public buildings designed by Sydney-based architect Peter Stutchbury, most notably in his design for the Sydney International Archery Park. There the roof twisted along its length, a dynamic slash above a wetlands landscape. Here in Newcastle, Australia's version of Glasgow or Liverpool, the parasol has a different role in the landscape. It provides a sheltering cleft in the slope of a hill overlooking a spectacular view of the Hunter River, the Stockton Bight and the city's shipyards and steelworks. The parasol was also a response to the protected 'heritage' view of the 19th century Bishop's residence which crowns Cooks Hill. Parameter and design strategy have been carefully conjoined.

The clients were a couple with four young children, and the brief was for a family home, with living spaces on the ground level and bedrooms above, all facing north towards the view. The house appears as a glassy pavilion, formal in plan with beautifully detailed timber box 'display cabinets' built into the window-wall. These 'cabinets' double as *brises-soleil* (shading devices) and provide privacy from the street below. As with all of Stutchbury & Pape's houses, there is a clear environmental agenda: the simple,

STUTCHBURY AND PAPE WITH BOURNE BLUE

1st floor bathroom

internal courtyard

1st floor corridor

relatively unadorned internal spaces of the house negotiate the double embrace of sun and vista. Nowhere is this negotiation more evident than within a double-height service court that lies deep in the plan and runs the full east-west length of the house. A slice cut into the parasol roof admits light to this crevasse of space, which has its walls shaded by vertical timber battens with shutter-like openings that fold outward. Behind this wall is a sequential run of baths, showers, toilets and basins which the female triathlete client describes as "the London Marathon of bathrooms". At night, the house takes on a completely different life: it becomes an exquisite domestic lantern, a dwelling beacon high above Newcastle's harbour.

PHILIP GOAD

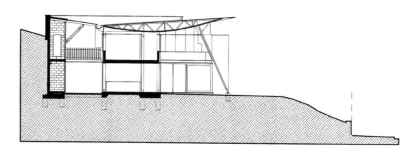

section

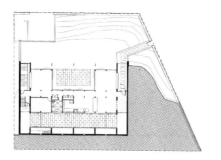

ground floor plan

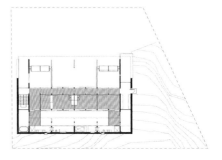

1st floor plan

north elevation

ADI PURNOMO

Urban House Jakarta, Indonesia 1997

view from north-west

< west elevation

Small houses in Indonesian housing estates are the most sought after yet problematic types. Typically, the houses are built as rows attached to one another, setting aside strips of land for front and back yards. Extensions commonly take place by building onto the back, producing compressed, poorly lit and ventilated spaces within an already dense neighbourhood.

Renovating one of these units in Pamulang, southwest of Jakarta, architect Adi Purnomo offers a critique of such flawed site planning and building design. Extending a small one-storey house into a much larger two-storey house, Purnomo comprehensively deals with climatic issues, lighting quality and functionality.

Central to the renovation is the creation of a core space in the form of a combined circulation area, staircase, skylight and air channel. Enclosed by a 10 metre high wall that divides the house into private and public zones, the core space is a device for passive climatic control within the house, connecting the coldest and the hottest air spots. Ventilation outlets, formed by hollowed cement blocks, are positioned on top of window and door openings to ensure connection between every room and the core air channel.

ADI PURNOMO

On ground level, a combined foyer and living area is positioned on one side of the wall, while on the other are a bedroom, bathroom and study. An open dining area links the two zones. As a breathing zone, a small courtyard is created adjacent to the dining room, bedroom and services area. Penetration of sunlight from the narrow skylight and front glass windows into the ground floor create a unique light and shade effect. On the upper level, a bedroom, bathroom and study area is positioned repeating the ground floor arrangement. A large void mediates the two levels.

Designed and built in 1996–1997, during the beginning of Indonesia's economic crisis, the architect effectively explored the use of low cost building materials and efficient construction, where finishing is kept to a minimum. The occasional use of white paint ensures brightness within the narrow interiors and visually widens the space.

Purnomo's experimentation, while meticulously produced to maximize the functionality and microclimatic quality of the narrow house, delivers a strong architectural statement through the cutting wall element. It slices though the climatically flawed continuous building rows. The wall visually disrupts this typical block of poor quality housing, an intervention crucially required by the majority of lower-middle class urban dwellers.

AMANDA ACHMADI

interior from ground floor

interior from 1st floor

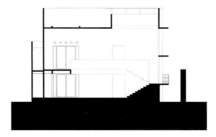

section

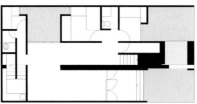

ground floor plan

1st floor plan

Urban House Jakarta, Indonesia 1997

west elevation

ARCHITECTURE WORKSHOP
(CHRISTOPHER KELLY)

Oriental Bay House Wellington, New Zealand 1997

view from south-east

< east elevation

Oriental Bay is a residential district immediately adjacent to downtown Wellington, with extensive views both of the city's CBD and its harbour. The Bay is backed by the northern flank of Mt Victoria, a prominent part of Wellington's topography, with the lower parts of the hillside densely covered by narrow timber houses interspersed with thick greenery and vertiginous streets and footpaths.

The Oriental Bay House nestles into this colourful mish-mash, not far up the hill but with its outlook as yet unimpeded by apartment blocks. The building is devised largely as a stack of five spaces, contained in staggered vertically repeated forms. Service spaces, storage and stairs are at the back of each. The house is clad in weathered plywood on its northern, most visible aspect. The walls on this stepped side lean back, as if in response to the city's notorious winds. Each level has on this face a shuttered door/window in the middle, opening onto the roof of the volume below. The house does not gulp down the wide northern views the way nearly all its neighbours do. Instead, it peeps. But it also looks cunningly along the hill to the east to find unexpected views: the building is extensively glazed on this less publicly visible side.

ARCHITECTURE WORKSHOP (CHRISTOPHER KELLY)

The language of the Oriental Bay House is far from that of the average New Zealand house. It could be considered a contemporary hybrid of the old vertical houses of inner Wellington, and the repeated apartment stacks now typical of the immediate neighbourhood. The house is intended to serve as a generous home for a couple with three children, and the lowest floor – the living area – has a higher ceiling than the others and a larger floor area. Like the next volume up, it opens onto a long, grassy terrace excavated out of the hillside. These two terraces will one day accommodate a pavilion, allowing an expansion of the house's principal living spaces. In this configuration, the accomplished play of repetition and difference, seclusion and exposure – hinted at in the house as it stands today – will become overt.

JUSTINE CLARK AND PAUL WALKER

ground floor

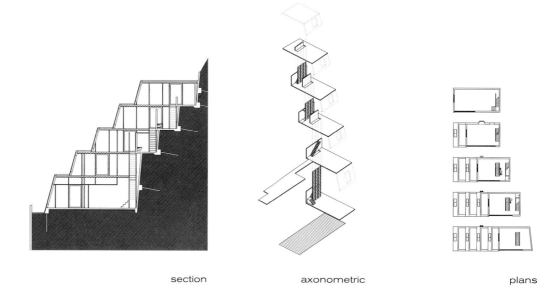

section   axonometric   plans

Oriental Bay House Wellington, New Zealand 1997

east elevation

SCDA ARCHITECTS

Andrew Road House Singapore 2002

Recent Singapore houses designed by Chan Soo Khian of SCDA demonstrate a distinctive language which grafts together several architectural approaches. The East Coast House (1996–2001) and the Coronation Road West House (1998) reveal a resolved composition of contrasting materials and forms. Textured wall planes combine with smoother surfaces, and robust stone walls are set against filigreed timber pavilions. A relentless orthogonal geometry is balanced by the dynamic roof-forms and incised openings in the walls. Such themes are continued in the Andrew Road House, with an initial dramatic view from the street of a flying cantilevered timber-clad box emerging from monumental anchored walls.

The house is essentially a small palace compound, where Japanese influence meets the minimalism and planar qualities of the Barcelona Pavilion by Mies van der Rohe. The dominant cantilevered timber-clad wing to the north-west contains the principal dining and entertainment areas, with bedrooms upstairs. A lower wing on

ground floor entry

ground floor entry >

the opposite side of the site is clad with a permeable metal screen and veiled internally with silvery drapes, presenting an ethereal vista when reflected in the swimming pool. The two wings are linked by a single-storey pavilion open on all four sides, which also serves as a reception area. The entry pathway from the street runs between two thick stone walls, and crosses over a softly splashing water feature. The entire compound engenders a feeling of tranquillity and decorum, where opulence has been discarded for a more satisfying rendition of serenity.

GEOFFREY LONDON AND
PATRICK BINGHAM-HALL

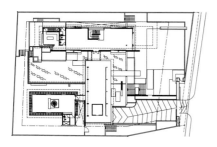

ground floor plan

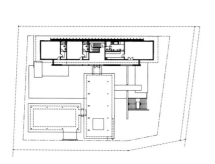

1st floor plan

south-east wing

view from south-west

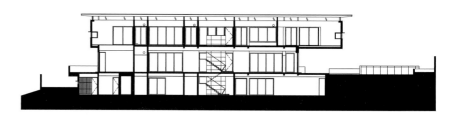

section

Andrew Road House Singapore 2002

view from street of north-west wing

SEKSAN DESIGN

Tempinis House Kuala Lumpur, Malaysia 1995–2003

Ng Sek San's own house and studio in the bustling Kuala Lumpur suburb of Bangsar has been evolving over eight years. The original two storey house was built in the 1960s, but has become the site of spectacular and spontaneous reinvention as a 'design test bed' for many of Seksan Design's projects. Alterations were originally made with timber, until it became clear that glass and steel were the way to go. Timber was assessed to be environmentally unsustainable, and the maintenance was too high. Shade trees planted in a porous garden floor outside the large glass doors have now matured, providing constantly cool conditions in a hot and sticky climate.

When Seksan Design began in 1994, a plan was set in place to spend 10% of company profit in support of local artists. Sek San explains this approach as "...a kind of paying back as I take a lot of inspiration in our works from 3D artwork, especially installations. We translate experimental installation into permanent landscaped public works". This inspired policy has resulted, ten years later, in a wonderful live-in art gallery, augmented by Sek San's own works. The large cane sculpture, wrapped with linen and paper, which twirls above the living room is designed

entry from street

kitchen from living room >

SEKSAN DESIGN

by Sek San and made by an Ipoh craftsman. Slightly less dextrous in execution is the doorway to the kitchen, smashed though an inconvenient brick wall by sledgehammer.

The renovation of existing housing stock in many Asian cities has become a fertile ground for architects and designers, and the Tempinis House has been transformed into an environmentally practical Aladdin's Cave. It is not a pure architectural exercise so much as a lesson in lifestyle, and in making a silk-purse from a sow's ear.

PATRICK BINGHAM-HALL

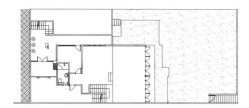

ground floor plan

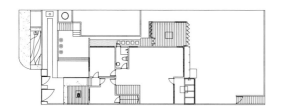

1st floor plan

ground floor living room

1st floor day room

Tempinis House Kuala Lumpur, Malaysia 1995–2003

ground floor living room

DONOVAN HILL

D House New Farm, Brisbane, Qld, Australia 2001

In Queensland, the architecture of Brian Donovan and Timothy Hill represents the exception rather than the rule. Unlike the previous generation of Brisbane architects who reinterpreted the elevated timber 'Queensland house' and explored the expressive potential of its pitched roof, the buildings of Donovan Hill have unusual aspirations. Monumentality (mass) is matched with 'the making of miniatures' through exquisite detail fragments (lightness). The entire site is re-inscribed as a potential architectural field; and the architects proffer a new spatial type for Brisbane's sub-tropical climate – the ventilating and open-air 'significant room' or space within a house.

The D House continues those themes and suggests possibilities for a model of medium-density housing in a sub-tropical suburban setting. But there is a twist to this. Donovan Hill are relaxed about their building's programmatic suppleness: "it may be used as a family house… but equally it may accommodate non-family residents, or someone working from home, with an independent office or studio; or it could be a shop, or a café…". Built in the street-facing backyard of an existing suburban lot that was subdivided and sold off, this modest two bedroom house is developed as if it were the

interior from north

street facade and entry from south >

walled garden of the existing house. The 'significant room' in this house is a long roofed terrace, glazed at either end with bedrooms and service rooms forming a thickened wall to the side boundary. It becomes, as the architects say, "a single continuous inside/outside space."

The house is alternately rich in tactility and crude in finish. This is deliberate: to reduce costs, but also to lavish care and to apply exquisite detail in the most significant points of the house. The rear bedroom and service zone was clad in timber cover strips, echoing the surrounding context of 19th century houses where the humble backside was usually a ramshackle collection on timber-clad skillion add-ons. By contrast, all the internal doors are 'heavy', veneered in timber with sophisticated soundproof seals and hand-crafted catches, rather than off-the-shelf handles. Experience is rewarded audibly and through touch. The ground plane has a variety of finishes that celebrate the idea of threshold: concrete, timber, pebbles, marble and water. A sliding timber screen, facing the street, can be drawn right back. From the built-in timber seat in the living room, one can then choose to live in a totally private world or in the semi-public front garden As in all Donovan Hill's work, an opening in the wall serves both as an engagement with and as a severance from the world outside.

PHILIP GOAD

west elevation

interior from south

section

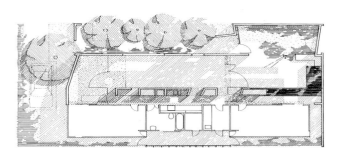

plan

D House New Farm, Brisbane, Qld, Australia 2001

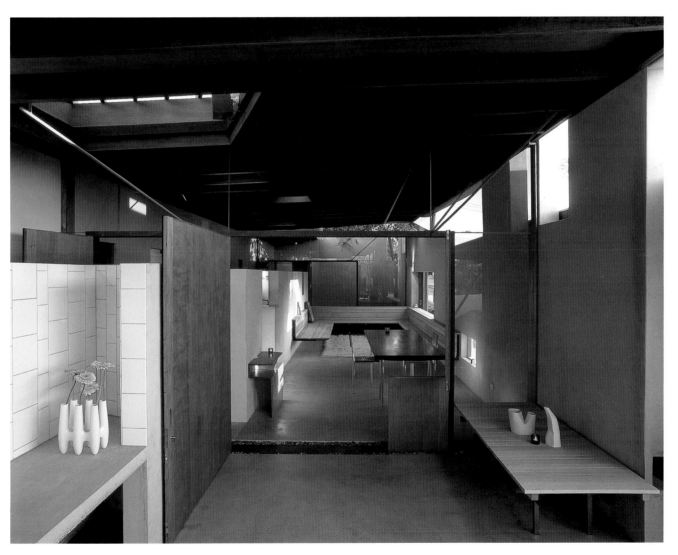

interior from north

AHMAD DJUHARA

Steel House Bekasi, Jakarta, Indonesia 2002

The 'Steel House' provides eloquent evidence for Ahmad Djuhara's argument that experimental design can offer optimal middle class housing despite constrained budgets and site limitations. The clients, a middle class couple with three children, requested the architect to explore design alternatives beyond the unaffordable though conventional 'concrete' house. The architect proposed the use of recycled industrial steel as the major building material, with compact spatial programming.

Ready-to-use steel beams and zincalume corrugated sheets produce smaller structural dimensions than the conventional concrete frame, thus creating more useable space and reduced costs. Considering steel's limited ability as a thermal buffer, the architect created a plenum, an air space between the roof and the ceiling, functioning as a heat barrier. The arrangement of openings allow cross ventilation, while a planted backyard improves the air quality. Instead of working with professional builders, Djuhara worked with the neighborhood's informal craftsmen, suggesting that those skills are available for further exploration by local architects.

1st floor

< north elevation

AHMAD DJUHARA

On the ground level of the three storey house, an open plan layout contains living, dining and kitchen areas, an uncommon solution for a society accustomed to rigid functional separation, particularly between the kitchen and living area. Djuhara argues that, with this multifunctional arrangement, a backyard garden can be created, contributing to a greater sense of space. The first floor contains the children's activities: individual bedrooms with a shared living area and bathroom. Each bedroom is equipped with an angular study area adjacent to a small window opening. On the second floor, an open plan layout contains the parent's living, sleeping and study areas, together with a bathroom.

Due to Jakarta's chronic transportation and planning problems, suburban dwellers spend most of the day away from their homes. It becomes common practice to employ servants to deal with house chores. Situated at the front part of the building is the servant's room and service area. Here, the service area is created as a healthy space, and is recognized as an important element of the house's maintenance and security control. This arrangement, as Djuhara states, 'returns' the backyard garden to the family, rejecting the common perception that the backyard is a 'backstage' area.

This experiment argues convincingly that common perceptions of housing in Indonesia can be critically challenged by means of design exploration.

AMANDA ACHMADI

ground floor from backyard

ground floor living room

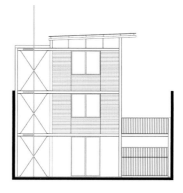

section

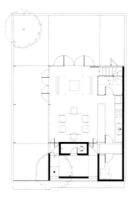

ground floor plan

1st floor plan

Steel House Bekasi, Jakarta, Indonesia 2002

view from south-east

SHYAMIKA SILVA

Nalin Indrasena House Nawala, Sri Lanka 1998–2001

Shyamika Silva works out of a small and relatively new practice in Sri Lanka with Christine Walbeoff. The Nalin Indrasena House, her first major work, captures the excitement and enthusiasm of a first journey, and offers both elements of delight and surprise.

A tall grey concrete cube is entered through a small doorway which accesses a dark corridor. At the end of the corridor, rounding a corner, is a triple height space that swells to fill the interior of the cube. An entire wall of the cube, which is three storeys high, has been opened up with a giant glass folding door and looks on the garden and a tall Jak tree. The only contained space is a small cantilevered bedroom on the upper floor, overlooking the main space. The simplicity of this soaring space, which allows comprehension of the entirety of the house reflects early Modernist experiments. Attention to detail, hidden sources of light and the flair with which a spiral staircase carries the eye upward through a skylight on to the flat rooftop soften the interior, allowing the large volume to be understood at a personal scale.

ground floor interior

north elevation >

SHYAMIKA SILVA

Silva built this cubic dwelling for her bachelor cousin, an aeronautical engineer who lives outside Sri Lanka. He found its simple program and pristine interior well-suited to his life-style. It was designed as a home to return to on his holidays, and is located next to his mother's old house, which dates back to the 1920s.

For Sri Lanka, Silva's design is an unusually daring excursion into minimalist design associated with a sophisticated Modern aesthetic. After finishing her schooling at the Colombo School of Architecture (SLIA) she spent a year studying urban design in Sydney at the University of NSW, and this exposure contributed tremendously to her developing ideas. However, in imagining and achieving them with the low cost technologies available to her in Sri Lanka, she had to develop innovative skills and a far sightedness that can only be learned on the job. The client was involved in the study of air movement throughout the house, enabling it to be naturally ventilated.

ANOMA PIERIS

entry corridor   living room from north

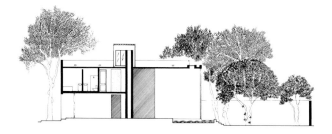
section

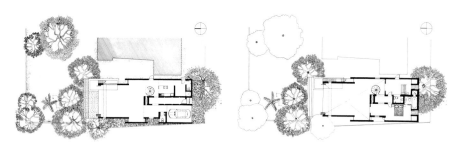
ground floor plan   1st floor plan

Nalin Indrasena House Nawala, Sri Lanka 1998–2001

living room from 1st floor

ANUPAMA KUNDOO

Anupama Kundoo House Auroville, Pondicherry, India 1999

Anupama Kundoo's own house in Auroville is a celebration of eco-friendly low cost technologies and energy saving methods. Her search over the years is rooted in the desire for a sustainable architecture which is carefully calibrated to respond to the impact of climate on a range of materials, and is derived from but improves upon local technologies. She is supported in this quest by the orientation of the Auroville community which strives for a symbiotic relationship with the natural landscape, and welcomes climatic changes as lived experience. Anupama studied in Bombay, and spent three years working in Berlin at Fiebelborn and Associates. She returned to Auroville in 1995 and is the chief executive of KOLAM, an architecture unit of Auroville, which engages in research, design and construction.

The house is designed as a high vaulted space flanked on either side by narrow private rooms - inhabited walls. A free-standing concrete staircase, painted green, rises alongside one wall and the structure is oriented to optimize air circulation.

Kundoo has experimented with a number of techniques and materials, including the use of local bricks laid with lime mortar to an ornamental

east elevation

vaulted main space >

ANUPAMA KUNDOO

pattern, which has eliminated the need for plastering, painting and tiling. The house boasts six roofing technologies aimed at reducing the use of steel and concrete. A series of shallow vaults have been built using hollow burned clay trapezoidal tubes assembled between trapezoidal beams. For internal concrete slabs that do not need insulation, burned clay pots are used as fillers, creating dome voids. They increase the effective depth and also reduce the volume of concrete. The floors in the private spaces are finished with timber from the short-living *acacia auriculiformis* trees of Auroville, and the flooring in bathrooms is of rough granite. Solar energy is utilised to meet all the electrical needs of the house, and to run a water-pumping system and water heater. Kundoo reiterates Auroville's policy of using local materials and village labour so as to reduce transportation and labour costs.

The house is a sensitive register of Auroville's climate so that local wind, rain and sun directions can be read in the articulation of spaces. In this house we find that rare sense of freedom with which an architect may delight in every material aspect of a built project, and shape it into an instrument of her own creative will.

ANOMA PIERIS

bathroom

internal staircase

section

section

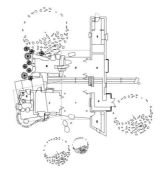

ground floor plan

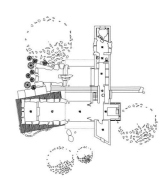

1st floor plan

Anupama Kundoo House Auroville, Pondicherry, India 1999

view from north

CY KUAN

Hardy House Sayan, Bali, Indonesia 1997

Commissioned by jeweller and decorative artist John Hardy and his wife Cynthia, this house perched high above the Ayung River in Sayan is a tribute to craft. The virtual tree-house was designed by CY Kuan, who orchestrated a dwelling that celebrates the warmth and energy of hand workmanship, and the richness of combining recycled timbers with as-found objects and traditional Balinese and Dutch Colonial furniture. There is expressed here a faith in the regenerative and innovative potential of examining centuries old techniques, not a tokenistic primitivism but a serious examination of the craft techniques that made lasting and practical contributions to building and dwelling.

Rather than interpreting the bale form (hipped roof pavilion) that is endemic to traditional Balinese architecture, or reproducing traditional carved ornament, or including fragments from older structures, CY Kuan, architect of the unique Begawan Giri Hotel near Payangan, went back to basics. The main house, linear in plan and part of a larger compound, is simply zoned: living spaces at ground level with sleeping above. The structural framing is unadorned post and beam timber, with real tree trunks added for extra

ground floor from north

view from north-east >

bracing. Man-made and natural branch braces work together. The spatial effect at the level of the living platform, which sits like a bridge over a pool, is that of a 'natural' architectural volume that might be formed by a grove of trees. What is actually a rigorously modulated structure appears softened by these inclusions. Even the additional timber props, that lend visual dynamism to the composition, appear utterly natural.

At the north end of the ground level platform is a screened dining room, the only concession to enclosure. Halfway along the length of the platform, a solid prop which is rendered in mud supports a timber stair. At a half landing there is a solid rampart-like pod roofed by a canopy of as-found sticks and white canvas, a tiny rustic belvedere from which to enjoy the breathtaking views of the gorge beyond. Woven grass matting, timber slats and shingles continue the crafted themes as the bedrooms and their balconies seem almost to merge with the trees. If one removed all the furniture, the objects of daily life from this house, there would remain a Spartan austerity, but also a primitive beauty derived from the natural imperfection of the stones, timbers and mud. The house has an elemental beauty that is of the hand and of nature – all life's encumbrances have been stripped away, so that one might dwell again in paradise.

PHILIP GOAD

east elevation

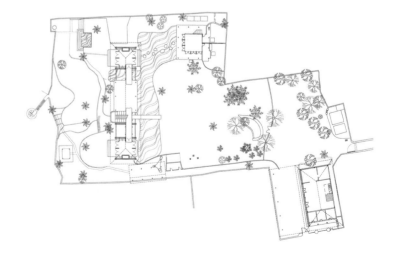

site plan

Hardy House Sayan, Bali, Indonesia 1997

ground floor from south

FEARON HAY

Rawhiti House Northland, New Zealand 1999

The Rawhiti House was commissioned by a client with long-standing family connections to the rural district where it is located. The site, in a small, isolated bay, slopes steeply down from the road and flattens out to face the water to the west. Along this edge of the site is a screen of pohutukawa – with twisted trunks and red summer flowers, these trees are conspicuous along the coast of northern New Zealand.

The house includes five bedrooms and a bunk room, service areas for diving and boating equipment, and extensive living areas with adjacent terraces. Open living areas are designed around a fireplace in a central glazed pavilion which has a terrazzo floor. Sleeping and service areas are located in the two enclosed volumes at both ends of the pavilion. These have gable roofs and are clad in dark aluminium, with matching aluminium louvres fitted over the glazing. The glass screens on the long sides of the central pavilion open to terraces on either side: the transparency allows visual connection to the water from the courtyard behind the house. The screens can be opened or closed to deal with different weather conditions.

Fearon Hay's usual architectural language is a contemporary adaptation of abstract Modernism. The gable-roof

west elevation from beach

west elevation >

FEARON HAY

forms of this house are transformations of existing sheds on the site. The owners already had a planning permit which allowed the sheds to be linked. Demolishing them and building from scratch would have entailed complying with new planning controls that required increased set-backs from the shoreline. The design took advantage of the earlier permit, reworking the sheds to make their forms disappear into the surrounding vegetation and connecting them with an elegantly proportioned glass box.

The conjunction of shed forms and the Neo-Modernist glass box also invites other readings. When making claims for an appropriate local architecture, architects in mid-20th Century New Zealand made strong links between the pragmatic buildings of early European settlers and the forms of Modernism. They argued that early settler buildings had a direct functional integrity they wished to emulate. Fearon Hay's house, built at the close of the 20th Century, pulls this history into focus again, inviting us to reflect on what the revival of such Modernist forms might mean now.

JUSTINE CLARK AND PAUL WALKER

ground floor from east courtyard

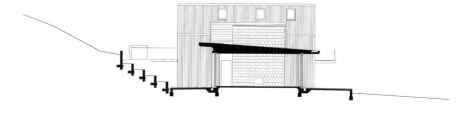

section

ground floor plan

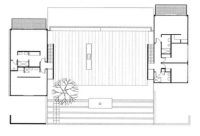

1st floor plan

Rawhiti House Northland, New Zealand 1999

west elevation

NGIOM PARTNERSHIP

Pat's House Sierramas, Sungei Buloh, Selangor, Malaysia 1995–1999

Lim Teng Ngiom set up his practice in 1989 after practising in London and with Kumpulan Akitek in Malaysia. His inspirations are from the early Modernism of Le Corbusier and Frank Lloyd Wright as well as Gordon Benson from Benson and Forsyth. He says "We like our architecture to be led by lyrical themes. Pat's House, for example is led by the idea of 'inflection', where forms are inflected to create experiences with light, i.e. what light does to our perception as forms are turned away or towards the observer. Inflected spaces also have an existential value, more varied than that in a simple box".

Pat's House is unusual if only because of its incongruity to its surroundings. Its simple Modernist lines contrast radically with its immediate neighbours. The house is located in a gated community of 'Chinese Tuscan' bungalows with hipped roofs. In the age of the 'Monster House', a return to simplicity is unimaginable for most suburban Malaysians, as borne out by derogatory comments about the house from neighbours: "Looks like a petrol station" (derogatory); "Looks like a shophouse" (joke); "Looks like a boat" (neutral); "If owners cannot afford a decent house, they should not be living here. Brings down value of surrounding properties" (malice).

east elevation

view from south-west >

NGIOM PARTNERSHIP

The client desired a low cost and ecologically sensitive house which could accommodate a working couple and her elderly mother. She was particularly concerned that the house should be "understated". In response to this brief, Ngiom designed a single storey house on a sloping site with a small guest area underneath. The plan and elevation, which are oriented north-south, shift almost imperceptibly to capture the changing tone of light over the day. The plan can be read as a single continuous space when all the doors and windows are open to the surrounding garden. The main floor has three bedrooms, which are connected by a canted corridor and lead to the cantilevered living and dining space. The living room broadens to maximize the view and has serried louvre windows on the east and west screening the interior from the low morning and evening sun. The service areas are in a small lower floor beneath the cantilevered southern end of the house.

Pat's House can be described as climate-sensitive Modernism. It has been designed with vents and louvres to maintain cross ventilation. The materials as described by Ngiom are "Concrete, steel, glass, air/space, earth, terrain, climate, commitment". In his view "form doesn't just follow function; it also follows lyrical intention"..

ANOMA PIERIS

ground floor corridor

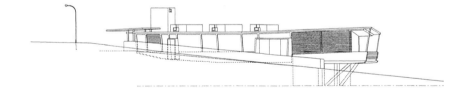

section

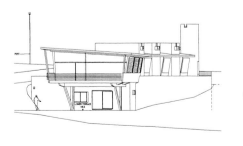

section

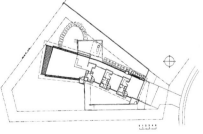

floor plan

Pat's House Sierramas, Sungei Buloh, Selangor, Malaysia 1995–1999

living area

TINAKORN RUJINARONG

Rujinarong's House Bangkok, Thailand 2003

A house designed for the architect and his family, but maybe more importantly a house designed for the architect's collection of chairs. Tinakorn Rujinarong has nearly two hundred individual chairs. He has chairs designed by Frank Lloyd Wright, by Gerrit Rietveld, by Charles Eames, by Charles MacIntosh, by Joseph Hoffman....and he even has designer bean bags.

Designed on an L-shaped plan, the two arms of the two-storey house enclose a tree-filled courtyard. Both internally and externally, the house is painted white, continuing the 1970s experiments of the New York architects known as 'The Whites'. Those architects, taking their cue from early Corbusier houses such as the La Roche House of 1923, typically designed white cubic structures featuring a lack of differentiation between surfaces such as walls and ceiling. Rujinarong's house updates this theme in reverence to the Modernist period which produced much of his family of chairs. Most of the ground floor of the main wing is a gallery for his chair collection,

south elevation from courtyard

dining room and vestibule >

TINAKORN RUJINARONG

and the dining table has many of Rujinarong's favourites. The gallery and the dining room are connected by a double-height void containing the foyer and staircase, with circular, triangular and rectangular windows admitting natural light. Private rooms for the family are upstairs.

PIRAK ANURAKYAWACHON

ground floor plan

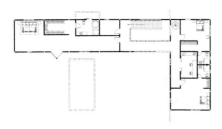

1st floor plan

Rujinarong's House Bangkok, Thailand 2003

dining room from east

TAN KOK MENG + LING HAO

Villa O Singapore 2001–2003

Kok Meng and Hao have always had a penchant for a self-reflexive architecture. The detail that absorbs them is the conscious and unconscious habits and quirks of human experience.

The Villa O is a two storey detached bungalow in Katong, eastern Singapore, designed for a Chinese businessman and his adult family. The architects have approached the project in a playful mood focusing on "aesthetic bodily experiences rather than conceptual notions of aesthetics". In keeping with this approach the project evolved its aesthetic during construction. Kok Meng describes how, on a trip to classical Chinese gardens in Suzhou, he was struck by the sensuousness of the experience: "gorgeous textures, meandering paths, static interiors, orchestrated views that unfolded as one moved around, sat on, looked at, walked under..."

The house has four levels. The architects, in keeping with the inspiration from China, describe them as different worlds. Starting from the basement, the den is a display area for the father's collection of antiques and memorabilia, and is painted white with curving walls and floors. It is "a seamless space" interrupted by the sound of a waterfall

1st floor

ground floor from north >

which brings light through a large void on the ground floor. Living spaces are on the ground floor and each are connected to different gardens through timber or glass sliding walls. The first storey is divided by a courtyard around which the bedrooms are designed as four private worlds, linked by an angled corridor painted electric blue and named 'the river of life'. The rooms are introverted (apart from a view of the sky), however when the translucent walls to the courtyard are open they connect the rooms to one another and to the street. The rooftop is approached by a steep stair with a bridge suspended over water and stones, (looking down on the river of life) and a dog-leg stair that opens up into a sky pavilion and roof garden. The entertainment facilities are housed in the southern half under a curved perspex or glass roof. The northern half is a garden where "you sit or lie down on circular bright green timber platforms wrapped by bonsais and creepers and count the stars".

The Villa O escapes categorization. It revives the mood of 1960s Swinging London and the Archi Zoom movement. It combines Zaha Hadid and Japanese pop de-materialism. But more importantly, while the rhetoric of Singapore architecture looks outward at its lost tropical geography, Kok Meng and Ling Hao look inward to an alternative landscape that craves liberation.

ANOMA PIERIS

ground floor plan

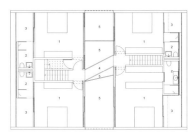

1st floor plan

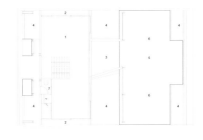

roof plan

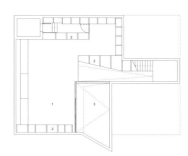

basement plan

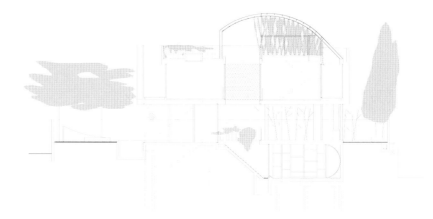

section

Villa O Singapore 2001–2003

roof

ground floor

ground floor bathroom

view from north-east

BLACKET SMITH

Victoria Park House Victoria Park, Perth, WA, Australia 2003

This intriguing house sits on a small 'battle-axe' site in inner suburban Victoria Park, just across the Swan River from the city of Perth. The architect owners, Rosanna Blacket and Des Smith, have produced a compelling example of their complex and intricate approach to architecture.

The house appears from its driveway approach to be a conventional brick and timber structure but as you move closer, it becomes apparent that something very different is going on. There are shifts and swellings in brick planes, textures and patterns. There is a precariously thin tent-like roof plane, and the sense of a purposeful lack of resolution in the composition.

The front door, a large pivoting sheet of glass, has clearly had a previous life, as have most of the materials comprising the house. The architects' preoccupation with recasting discarded materials has resulted in a highly inventive building. Working with Frank's Salvage Yard, sympathetic to the project, used materials have been collected over a period of time, directed by design intentions but also allowing these intentions to be shifted by what treasures turned up. This demanded a nimble response to the circumstantial nature of as-found materials. Once regarded as luxurious, the discarded

ground floor living room and stairs

view from north >

BLACKET SMITH

materials – granite, marble and timber – are reinvested with value. The architects suggest a parallel with the Byzantine practice of using Roman 'junk' in their buildings.

18 tonnes of timber was bought from a disused abattoir. Lanoline-soaked timber from the skin drying racks was dressed to 40 x 40 square sections, laminated into blocks, and laid as flooring in patterns which, in seeking a uniquely Australian quality, respond to those found in Aboriginal paintings. Larger sections of timber were cleaned up and used in the structure, but not to the extent that their previous roles can't be recognised.

The house is overflowing with incident, with junctions articulated and providing opportunities for rich formal experiment. The design rejects the possibility of a 'whole', and remains open and flexible, with independent identities for each element, resulting in the boundary between inside and outside being blurred and ambiguous.

The roof shape, developed from folded paper, controls the push and shape of rooms. Interior volumes are carefully massaged, and their skin is very inconsistent, with edges of materials exposed and layered. Fragile plastic, glass and metal sheets are contrasted with muscular brickwork and over-scaled steel structure. The house itself is a celebration of the process of architecture, thoroughly drawn and understood. It is a house that will continue to evolve with its own vigorous trajectory.

GEOFFREY LONDON

stairway from 1st floor

living room detail

section

ground floor plan

1st floor plan

Victoria Park House Victoria Park, Perth, WA, Australia 2003

view from west

KEVIN LOW

Kevin Low House Kuala Lumpur, Malaysia 2000

Kevin Mark Low began to renovate a 1950s row house in the Bangsar area in early 2000, while he was working for GDP Architects in Kuala Lumpur. He has since started his own company, designing "small projects", which focus on garden houses. His practice is characterized "by an entirely uncorporate identity". Says Kevin, "Small projects refers not to the size of things but to the intimate relationship that narrative shares with space and detail. It is about the possibility of context".

Low's own house is best experienced in the quiet of the evening when the tropical twilight sharpens its colours and textures. The main source of his inspiration was the weathered unfinished clay brick walls of the neighbouring TNB storage yards, with this same texture recreated for the new walled garden. The house is entered through a breach in the high garden wall past a screen of saplings and under a thin concrete blade roof. The entrance door slides left to reveal a richly hued and intimate garden-space with a patio at the far end. Inside, loose gravel, a ficus triangularis and a frangipani tree become integral to the spatial experience of the ground floor. A cherry tree planted outside the wall spreads its slender boughs over the far

entry area from house

courtyard from studio >

corner. The path through the garden leads to the patio/outdoor dining area, which is under another thin concrete roof and looks onto a patch of lawn. Pools of light filter into the interior through tall forest trees planted in a courtyard at the rear. When contrasted with the pristine and finished quality of the current 'tropical architecture' trend, this approach is arresting for its subtlety and texture.

The project grew incrementally with the use of a number of sub-contractors. Says Low, "I designed the renovation to disguise bad finishing, poor workmanship and cheap finishes". He worked through a series of sketches and designs, which he communicated directly to the workmen.

For Low, the idea of a garden house predominates. He feels most strongly about Modern architecture "which shows the passing of time, like a garden, like a landscape." He feels that Modern architecture should be always unfinished: in his view, "time completes it". Inside and outside are seen as different rooms in a house where textures are carefully calibrated to satisfy issues of maintenance and practicality and to allow for the passage of time. In his interpretation, time itself takes on a tactile quality that has long been considered inimical to Modernist experiments.

ANOMA PIERIS

courtyard from studio

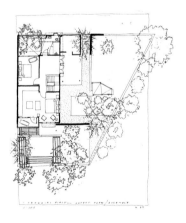

ground floor plan

1st floor plan

Kevin Low House Kuala Lumpur, Malaysia 2000

dining area

studio from courtyard

dining area from courtyard

dining room

VIJITHA BASNAYAKA

Maulie De Saram House Pelwatte, Battaramulle, Sri Lanka 2000

street elevation

< view to entry from living area

Vijitha Basnayaka has always worked in the spirit of the bricoleur. He remains unswayed by the picturesque ideology of regionalism, and aims instead to give reign to what he describes as the inherent character of the material and tectonic, and while he draws his inspiration from Western architects, he stresses the importance of regional influences, and local vernacular architecture and landscapes.

Basnayaka's architecture is forged from the intensification of a particular mood created for each client. In the case of Maulie De Saram it is a 'windowless home' that draws on the dark protective qualities of introverted space particular to traditional cultural experiences. Basnayaka describes two key inspirations: the dark entrance into the cave-like monastic complex at Maligathenne which opens up into a brightly lit garden; and the idea of false perspective from Palladio's Teatro Olimpico in Vicenza. Likewise on the triangulated and sloping site in Pelwatte, a suburb of Colombo, the built space forms a dark barrier that must be penetrated to enter the brightly lit garden-living spaces that unfold within. The house is designed as two units which fully explore the quality of space and light on the site. There are no clear demarcations of spatial boundaries and, due to the

VIJITHA BASNAYAKA

unfinished quality of the recycled materials, the lived-in space blends with the roughness of the natural terrain. The use of natural pigments from vegetable compounds enhances the colour and texture of the interior, and the un-interrupted flow of interior surfaces gradually merges with the sand and river-stone exterior, emphasising the particular quality of openness and freedom sought by the client. Careful landscaping and terraced areas exaggerate the perspective of the garden.

Basnayaka's interest in integrating the lived and garden spaces comes from a rejection of the artificial boundaries maintained in temperate climates. While he interprets the vernacular as an organic and spontaneous response to needs and desires, he also tests the limits of engineering and remains quite uninhibited by the norms of formal architecture practice. Consequently his conception of space has always displaced conventional notions of inside/out, built/un-built or the act of middle-class dwelling itself, to venture defiantly into new and experimental idioms.

Basnayaka's detailed knowledge of both his craft and his modern inspirations enable innovation and experiment and make possible a contemporary application of the vernacular, rooted in the pleasure of everyday and familiar textures, colors and sensations. Consequently, his experimental method renders the ordinary extraordinary in a provisional and changeable architecture.

ANOMA PIERIS

kitchen

living area

section

floor plan

Maulie De Saram House Pelwatte, Battaramulle, Sri Lanka 2000

indoor/outdoor living area

CLINTON MURRAY WITH SHELLEY PENN

Overcliffe Potts Point, Sydney, NSW, Australia 2002

view from north-east

< east elevation from rear laneway

This project demonstrates an exemplary solution to the potential conflict between urban renewal and heritage controls. It was initially intended to be a completely new house on the site of an old timber cottage. However, the local authority, having earlier given approval for demolition, determined that the cottage had heritage value and should be retained.

The clients were seeking qualities associated with a new house rather than a renovated old house – open space, light, direct garden connection and security. Clinton Murray had designed a new house to meet these expectations, and was now faced with the requirement to work with the old house. He resolved this dilemma by exposing it, and converting the meeting of the new and old into an eventful architectural junction.

Murray had previously worked with a group of trades-people with whom he'd developed trust and respect. This allowed him to resolve details on site and work directly with the materials and the problems they presented. This approach was not possible for the Potts Point project, so Murray invited Shelley Penn, someone whose detailing he admired, to collaborate with him. Murray's work, tough and focused on

CLINTON MURRAY WITH SHELLEY PENN

surface richness, now combined with Penn's more delicate approach, concerned with light and volume. The result is a very polished conversion of an old mariner's cottage.

Recycled wharf timber is used to create a crisply detailed two-storey 3D frame structure, with solid and glazed infill panels fixed within the frame. Reflecting the two architectural approaches there is a strong contrast between the rough, over-scaled timber frame and the fineness of the new timber and interior detailing. On the ground floor, the north-facing glass wall to the garden is independent of the frame, moving inwards and outwards, with the floor surfaces extending into the luxuriant garden and making it part of the new living room. In a dense urban setting, surrounded by blocks of apartment buildings, the architects have achieved a high level of privacy while still allowing open-ness and light.

GEOFFREY LONDON

view from south-east

living area from cottage

section

1st floor bedroom

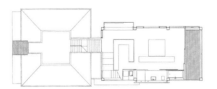
1st floor plan

ground floor plan

Overcliffe Potts Point, Sydney, NSW, Australia 2002

view from north-east

CHAN SAU YAN ASSOCIATES

Tupai House Singapore 2000–2002

front garden and living area

< staircase from 1st floor

Chan Sau Yan (Sonny Chan) set up practice in Singapore in 1993 as Chan Sau Yan Associates and has struck a strong balance between teaching and practice, benefiting from what he describes as a tripartite relationship between practitioners, academics and students. His previous projects have been unusual for their undulating copper roofs and experimental forms. The Tupai House is an interesting departure from his customary aesthetic in what may well be a new direction in his architecture.

Sonny describes the project as representative of a Modernistic direction in the residential field taken by his practice, which was hitherto regional in its design focus. In his view it also expresses a trend where clients have become increasingly accepting of Modernist traditions. Local Modernism, in his view, must "avoid falling into the debased International Style trap and produce architecture which is modern and tropical". Similarly he has taken care to avoid the commodified tropical style which is circulated through traditional or vernacular images typical of cultural tourism. For example although the client's initial request was for a Balinese style house he was "subsequently convinced that a

CHAN SAU YAN ASSOCIATES

modern contemporary house was more appropriate for the site".

The design parti is a simple box, which is glazed and transparent at the ground floor living areas and is wrapped in a seamless perforated cladding at the upper bedroom level. The open plan and a skylight over the central staircase, which leads to the roof garden terrace, heighten the transparency of the living areas. A glazed bridge on the first floor allows light to filter down from the skylight into the entrance vestibule. High level horizontal slit windows, screened terraces and louvred panels in timber or glass vary the quality of light on the upper level. The set backs around the box are landscaped, giving it a green edge of lawn, bamboo and pebbled court while the entrance is flanked by a water garden with a screen wall of dried ferns and parasitic plants.

With the Tupai House, Sonny Chan has explored a minimalism equivalent to the Modern Japanese aesthetic he so admires. He observes that the early Japanese architects who captured a Japanese identity in a new interpretation of Modernism "liberated from Western imagery" impressed him, and interested him in developing a similar sensibility for a tropical climate. While his design does not cater to the nostalgia of tropical living, its extroversion, transparency and simple pragmatism responds directly to its context and climate.

ANOMA PIERIS

dining area from 1st floor

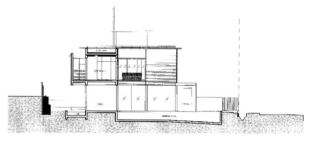

section

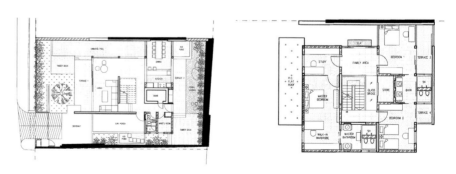

ground floor plan   1st floor plan

view from south-west

DONOVAN HILL ARCHITECTS

N House Ascot, Brisbane, Qld, Australia 2003

south-west wing from east

< lantern and entry from south

The N House is the latest in a series of houses by Brian Donovan and Timothy Hill that carry a cryptic alphabetical label, suggesting that they're part of a larger experiment, the testing of prototypes. The architectural outcomes reinforce that view with the utilisation of recurring and evolving design strategies. These are propositions for enlightened living in Australian suburbia, overlain with the particular conditions of sub-tropical Queensland, and unleashing the armoury of a highly skilled and creative architectural partnership.

On a steep slope, the N House follows the strategy of fully occupying the site, of designing the whole site rather than just the building placed upon it. This creates an almost civic scale to the complex, a monumental enclosure with a large landscaped court providing the foreground to spectacular views to the Brisbane CBD, and a series of spatially choreographed approaches to the house.

The planning of the house allows for what the architects describe as 'household adjustment'. It has the flexibility, privacy and range of access options to allow occupation by a single family, to be shared, or to be a place of living and working.

DONOVAN HILL ARCHITECTS

The solid shell of the L-shaped house, backing into a corner of the site, has a screen of timber filigree to the south-west corner, forming a double volume outdoor room. The major internal rooms are formed in a series of linked layers with carefully controlled views and lighting, varying degrees of intimacy, and all with large glazed sliding doors that control the degree of enclosure.

It is a house which has an arcane quality, with a setting suggestive of ritual events which, together with the fragmentary nature of the architecture and the ambiguity between contained and interior space, contributes to the sense of a grand inhabited landscape.

GEOFFREY LONDON

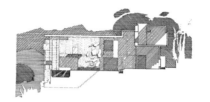

section

section

courtyard entry from east

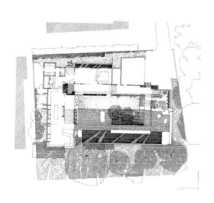

ground floor plan

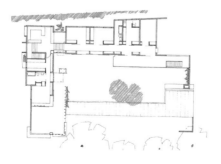

1st floor plan

interior of south-west wing

N House Ascot, Brisbane, Qld, Australia 2003

living room

BOONLERT HEMVIJITRAPHRAN

Vit Vattanayothin's House Bangkok, Thailand 2002

dining area

< south elevation

The patrician and elegant house for Vit Vattanayothin takes its architectural form from the traditional colonial residence. But Boonlert Hemvijitraphran has integrated functionality with the harmony of the understood colonial form and with the beautiful garden. The architect is deeply attuned to methods of construction, and with this house he chose to utilize the accuracy and uncompromising rigour of metal structure as opposed to timber or masonry. Vertical folding metal louvres surround the glass walls of the house on both levels, a double skin which encourages excellent ventilation and cooling.

The entrance to the house leads to a staircase and a series of peaceful rooms, culminating in a double-height dining room. This dining room can be segregated from the other rooms with a series of hinged panels, echoing the external louvre system. The upstairs bedrooms are cooled by the double skin external walls, and by a double layer roof plane of metal and concrete. The house is enabled to breathe by the raising of the ground floor by one and a half metres above the garden.

BOONLERT HEMVIJITRAPHRAN

This neo-colonial style villa presents
an intriguing prototype in a country that
was proudly never colonized. But colonial
architecture was a graceful and practical
style throughout tropical Asia, and this
house for Vit Vattanayothin reintroduces
this beautiful architectural type in a
practical way for the 21st Century.

PIRAK ANURAKYAWACHON

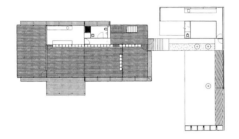

ground floor plan

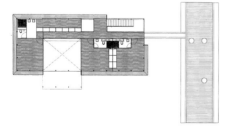

1st floor plan

elevation

Vit Vattanayothin's House Bangkok, Thailand 2002

view from south-east

MITCHELL AND STOUT

Waitamariki House Northland, New Zealand 1998

entry from south

< view from south

The Bay of Islands, 250km north of Auckland, is an impossibly beautiful location relatively unblemished by human intrusion. The Waitamariki House is embedded in the crown of a spur protruding into the southern shore of the bay. It forms part of a discreet enclave which is only visible from the water. This determined the architectural strategy for the site. The house was designed to fit in with the surrounding landscape, not to dominate, and not to interrupt the line of the hill when seen from the water. A piece of land sculpture has evolved, with long stone walls extending beyond the edges of the house. These retaining walls, built from Hinuera stone, appear to compress the house into the ground, creating enclosure and sanctuary. Viewed from the south, the house can be construed as a bunker (providing a number of connotations for 21st Century living).

Within this hillside sanctuary, vaulted pavilions look out to the panoramic view through slatted screens, breaking the vista into fragments. Framed views of the sky above are as deliberately composed as the views to the north, encouraging a more diverse engagement between the inhabitant and the natural environment. The architects had the romantic notion of

MITCHELL AND STOUT

a simple shelter set amongst the 'ruins' in long grass. This romantic imagining applied to building in paradise subverts the continuing desecration of much of the New Zealand coastline, with new settlement so crude and prominent that it actually becomes the 'view'. David Mitchell and Julie Stout are, conversely, working towards a kinetic relationship between the building, the human being and the landscape.

PATRICK BINGHAM-HALL

living room

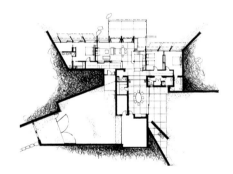

floor plan

driveway entry from west

Waitamariki House Northland, New Zealand 1998

view from north-east

section through hillside

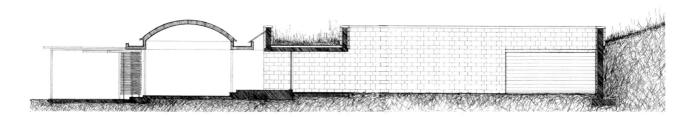

section

Waitamariki House Northland, New Zealand 1998

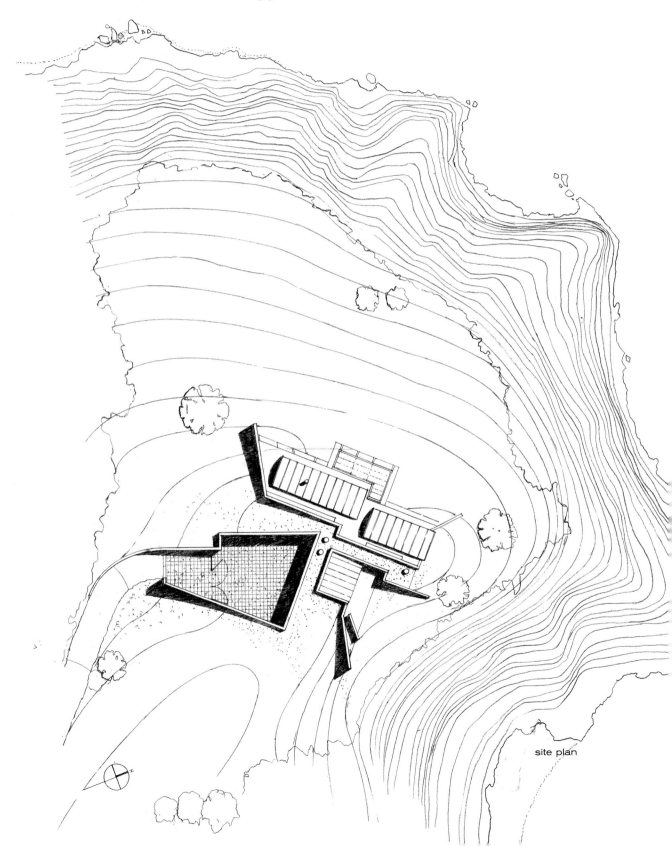

site plan

SEAN GODSELL

Peninsula House Mornington Peninsula, Vic, Australia 2002

For Melbourne architect Sean Godsell, every new house represents an opportunity to build on earlier themes, continuing experiments in "making something out of nothing." Yet Godsell also declares that every new house bears the "thumbprint of its owners and is completely different from all the others". The client for this house had been impressed by Godsell's own house, Kew (1998), a rusted steel box on a sloping site, and his Carter/Tucker House, Breamlea (2000), a horizontally-battened timber beach box edged into a dune. Each has a corridorless plan and an adjustable shading skin that develops patina as it weathers.

The site for the Peninsula House is also behind a dune, with a surf beach just fifty metres away. The brief was to provide a calm and relaxed retreat that might be lived in three or four days of the week. It had to "be about the beach", easy to maintain and unobtrusive from the sandy laneway. It is exactly that, and the house greets the laneway as a humble car-port backed by a blank rusted steel wall and two steel doors.

view from south-east

view from north-west >

SEAN GODSELL

On opening the right hand steel door, one enters the magical world of a filigreed timber box. The entire house is clad in thin strips (eight kilometres!) of recycled jarrah, a Western Australian hardwood. The timber slats are undressed, some are slightly twisted, and the house has a coarse outer hide that completely covers its two longest sides and roof. Inside however, the effect is one of extreme delicacy. The skin's uneven quality means that sunlight "forces its way in", or as Godsell says "light spits, even splinters itself into the building." Within, the tectonic rationale becomes clear: a gridded frame of rusted steel, a bend in the frame to accommodate a giant gutter, a glass roof, and the sheath of timber slats. From the double-height living room, one discovers a hidden study/second bedroom; a secret stair on the other side of a blank white wall that leads upstairs to the master bedroom; and from there a bathroom court, and a outdoor shower room. There are more surprises: whole panels of the timber slats fold up to reveal a barbecue court complete with rusted steel chimney. There is experiential delight in circumambulating this plan. Monumental form is complemented by an interior of Loosian complexity. This is a house that, as Godsell says, "can be unpacked".

PHILIP GOAD

east barbecue area and passageway   south courtyard

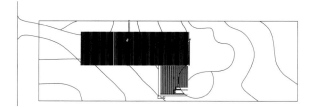

site plan

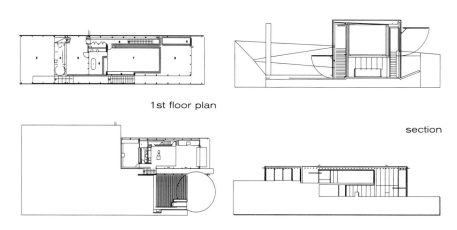

1st floor plan   section

ground floor plan   section

Peninsula House Mornington Peninsula, Vic, Australia 2002

view from north-east

HIRANTI WELANDAWE

Manel Nivasa House Colombo, Sri Lanka 2000–2003

entry from west

< living area from west

Hiranti Welandawe's influences include study at the University of Moratuwa and in Scandinavia, a combination that has shaped some of Sri Lanka's most avant garde architecture. However, she attributes her training under Stein Doshi & Bhalla and her work in architectural practices in Finland for her particular approach. Welandawe combines a lecturership at the Colombo School of Architecture with private practice. She says that her work has been "largely affected by the transformations in Sri Lankan society in the past few decades – socialist policies, open economy and new technologies". As a result, her work has focused on developing a contemporary and essentially Sri Lankan language.

What is striking about the Manel Nivasa House is its austerity, reminiscent of the *maduwas* (storage structures) seen in many Singhalese villages. This project declares its loyalty to the vernacular with its emphasis on local materials, and by refusing the manicured finish of the popular minimalist trend. The house is organized as two high shed-like spaces: the sleeping wing and the living wing, which are placed on either side of a shallow pool designed to cool the entire house.

HIRANTI WELANDAWE

Welandawe observes that within these containers the experience of interior spaces is governed by the Singhalese idea of 'ambiguity', expressed by the word *nikang*–(no meaning /no definition) which captures the laid back and accommodating temperament of an anti-hierarchic rural Buddhist culture. Hence only the sleeping and service areas of the house have been defined; the rest flow in to each other and from inside to outside, creating spatial ambiguity. The hall can be used as a lounge, dining or workspace; or informal eating could take place in the lounge, poolside or in the office room. The dining table doubles as a workspace, while the office room can be used as a bar, if male guests chose to consume alcohol in private according to the rural tradition.

Welandawe acknowledges that the client, S. Bandaragoda, his wife Manel and their thirteen year-old son have been the main source of inspiration. Whereas her mainstream clientele are the cosmopolitan English speaking elite who come from middle and upper middle-class backgrounds, S. Bandaragoda stands out as a self-made businessman who remains rooted to his Singhala-Buddhist and rural origins. His unapologetic attitude toward his own socio-cultural identity was a key source of inspiration to Welandawe. Unlike most examples of vernacular-derived architecture in which the aesthetic supports an elite nostalgia for lost experiences, Hiranti's design captures the psychological comfort of her client's actual socio-cultural habitus.

ANOMA PIERIS

living area from west

living area from east

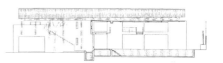

section

ground floor plan

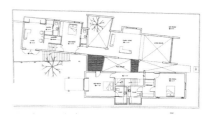

1st floor plan

Manel Nivasa House Colombo, Sri Lanka 2000–2003

living area

DOMINIC DUBE

Inge's House Auroville, India 2003

1st floor

< view from east

Dominic Dube arrived in Auroville in 1996 after working for three years with the Indian architect Balakrishna Doshi. His initial training was in Quebec, then in Rome, until he "fell in love with India" ten years ago. He started a studio named 'Brand New Day' which explores an innovative approach he describes as being somewhere between school and practice.

Inge's House is striking for its sculptural quality, expressing the plasticity of concrete as a construction material. Both the concrete and the black stone, which is either sedimented or polished, emphasise the formal elements of Dominic's architecture. The house itself stands in the landscape as a tall pavilion, yet is integrated both by its openness to its surroundings and by the shallow pools in which it rests. The main spatial expression of Inge's House is in the double height living area which acts as dining room and kitchen. The most secluded area is the internal bath courtyard with walls of orange tiles.

Inge's interest in Zen Buddhist philosophy and a desire to be integrated with her surrounding environment has had a strong influence on Dube's design. The brief called for tranquility and harmony with the natural context. However, the spaces were designed to be flexible to capture the fluidity and motion of lived-experience, by relying on the structure itself to define spatial boundaries and by ignoring the functional separation of rooms. A secondary structure of local brick covered with Venetian-style stucco and an extremely glossy patina, screens and softens the quality of the internal spaces. A freestanding spiral stair descends from above like a twisted ribbon, and the polished surfaces reflect and refract light from the external pools and through the glazed areas.

Inge's House encapsulates Auroville's legacy as a context for utopian experiments in space, form and engineering. Here, Dube's architecture is able to explore alternative definitions of space and life-style that appear futuristic in their rural setting. In addition, the house has a tectonic quality earned through the careful placement and jointing of building elements so as to preserve the integrity of form and structure. Above all, Dube is philosophical about his approach and observes that air, water, nature and moreover, love and respect for the creative process, are the major materials he uses in construction.

ANOMA PIERIS

view from north

west elevation

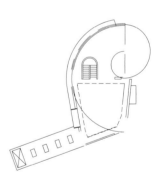

1st floor plan

ground floor bathroom

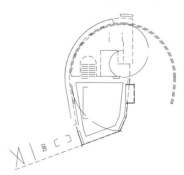

ground floor plan

Inge's House Auroville, India 2003

1st floor

DANIEL SANDJAJA

Coba House Denpasar, Bali, Indonesia 2001

Entering Daniel Sandjaja's house is like entering a living room opened to the sky. The project is distinctive for its careful mediation between the inside and the outside, for its adaptation of Modern architectural forms in the tropical climate, and for instigating the reworking of indigenous architectural traditions beyond stylistic reproduction. Situated in Denpasar, the forgotten city of the culturally charged island of Bali, the project proposes that architectural forms produced by specific regions should not be read as a final solution, nor should they dictate architectural identification. The Coba House, a 'trial' house built as the architect's own residence, argues that forms are created, neither as stylistic reproduction nor as essentialized architectural identity, but as the means and result of design investigation.

The strength of the multi-pavilion dwelling form, indigenous to rural Bali, is that it produces a breathing shelter, protected yet touched by nature. Learning from this, Sandjaja deconstructs the common walled-in house form by emptying one modular unit at the centre of the building's structural grid, creating a central courtyard and a backyard. This leaves two volumes at the front and rear of the site, visually and physically connected

internal courtyard

< east elevation

by the courtyard and two passages alongside, functioning as an enclosed bathroom and design studio on the ground floor, and as semi-open corridor spaces connecting the two bedroom units on the upper level. A staircase from the corridor leads to a rooftop viewing platform on top of the rear volume.

The taller rear volume channels air through the courtyard into the building. The backyard and the external façade, which is covered by hollowed cement blocks, ensure continuous airflow. The external façade of the front volume provides setbacks and overhangs to protect the house from monsoon rainfall and the harsh tropical sun. In contrast, the internal façades are enclosed with sliding aluminum framed glass doors, creating a maximum transparency. The interiors unfold as one vast flowing space. Combined ventilation and skylight units on the rooftops substitute for the traditional role of the pitched-roof ceiling space in channeling out hot air.

While Modern architectural forms have long been considered unsuitable for Indonesia's climate, and while stylistic reproduction of Balinese architecture has often displaced architectural exploration, Sandjaja's work repositions architecture as place making. Form making is treated as a means to explore an optimum formula of built environment sensitive to the climate and the inhabitant's mode of living.

AMANDA ACHMADI

ground floor plan

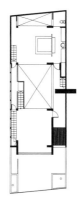

1st floor plan

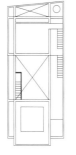

2nd floor plan

view from west tower

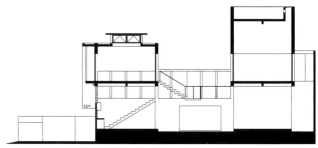

section

Coba House Denpasar, Bali, Indonesia 2001

1st floor from east

JANE WETHERALL AND GEOFFREY WARN (DONALDSON + WARN)

Glick House Leederville, Perth, WA, Australia 1999

The Glick House, a semi-industrial box framed within a rusting steel structure, is defiantly different from the surrounding inner suburban cottages. The house was designed for an artist whose work shows an ongoing fascination with assemblages of low-level industrial equipment. This, together with the artist's attraction for the as-found engineering aesthetic of an old foundry, overlapped creatively with the architects' interests, determining their approach.

The small site and the constraints imposed by the local authority impinge powerfully on the building. The house is extruded upwards: the artist's studio on the ground floor, his residence on the first floor, and, sitting within the deep band of the roof fascia, is a roof deck (the displaced patio). All are accessed by an external stair with handrails of scaffolding-like tubular steel. The disposition of the windows is determined, to an extent, by the requirement that views into neighbouring backyards be restricted. A high strip of glazing wraps around the building, and separates the roof from the walls. The fascia is clad in a translucent plastic which is lit from behind and glows at night, giving the house a space ship quality - an alien visitor hovering in the suburbs.

view from south-west

staircase from north-west >

JANE WETHERALL AND GEOFFREY WARN
(DONALDSON + WARN)

The building provides the kind of living/working relationship, the artist house/studio, that was a point of departure for the early utopian projects of Le Corbusier. For him, as is the case in the Glick House, the process of everyday living was to be elevated to a higher plane, lifted out of the mundane, becoming a celebration that offers a critique of convention. The living floor of the Glick House is split into three levels, resulting in each of the functions of eating/dining, living and sleeping/bathing having their own stage for enactment.

In the toughness and directness of this building there is a challenge to the complacency and predictability that can be found in suburban living. The roof deck, raw and utilitarian, opens the house up to the vast blue sky of Perth. This, together with the candid exposure of the house to the street, is an extroverted action as opposed to the suburban convention of turning inward, gestures borne of a fear of the urban world.

Geoffrey Warn and Jane Wetherall, together with key contributions from the artist, Rodney Glick, and his engineer father, have forged an unrelentingly hard-edged building, pragmatically determined and detailed, a persuasive model for an alternative approach to living and working in the suburbs.

GEOFFREY LONDON

south elevation

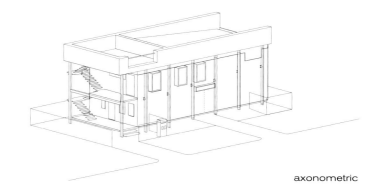

axonometric

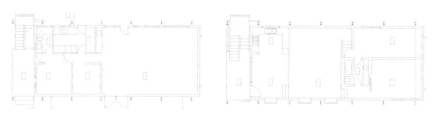

ground floor plan   1st floor plan

view from south-west

ARCHITECTURE WORKSHOP
(JAMES FENTON)

Wakefield Street Apartments Wellington, New Zealand 2000

The Wakefield Street Apartments in central Wellington are a roof-top addition to an old commercial building, which was not particularly distinguished in its own right but significant as part of a district with a distinct and consistent built character.

The architects have asserted a formal language for the apartments completely different from that of the commercial building on which they sit. Architecture Workshop and the client explored several earlier designs that contained the apartments under a barrel-vault or a lamella structure roof. The built version articulates them as three row-houses, each of two storeys, which take the roof of the existing building as a new ground plane. Entry to each apartment is from a shared open space, forming a small pedestrian 'street' at this datum. The new work is carefully detailed to make overt its mode of construction, thus distinguishing itself from the old building, but also from the rash of poorly conceived recent rooftop additions in Wellington that try unsuccessfully to hide or 'blend-in' with the existing built fabric. The row-house strategy, as opposed to stacked loft-like spaces, allows for a degree of volumetric play within each apartment, and the architects have taken full advantage of this.

view from south-east

view from north-east >

view from south-east

Wakefield Street Apartments Wellington, New Zealand 2000

The Wakefield Street Apartments explicitly claim inner city Wellington as their site. They deal with their relationship to the city by placing themselves overtly within it. The corner apartment, in particular, flaunts its architecture in a very public location, directly opposite a car park that serves one of New Zealand's most affluent supermarkets. The glassy walls of the apartment allow everyone to see its interior, the art on the walls, and the chairs around the dining table. At night it becomes a kind of domestic light-box, or a magic lantern.

JUSTINE CLARK AND PAUL WALKER

view from north

view from north-west

living area

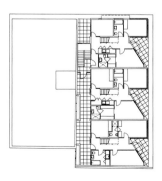
3rd floor plan

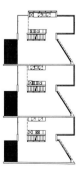
4th floor plan

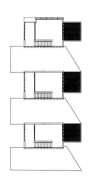
5th floor plan

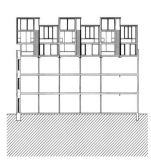
section

PORNCHAI BOONSOM

MnG House Bangkok, Thailand 2001

This unlikely and exciting project sitting in a typical suburban Bangkok street combines office space and a home for a family with young children. The main stairway connects all the spaces in the house and creates constant interactive movement. The design imperative was to integrate walls, floors and ceilings as one piece of flowing planar surface.

The design of this house, as with much of Pornchai Boonsom's work, involves movement and replacement – a reaction, which the architect describes as "motion in four dimensions". This involves the movement between man and architecture through a series of spaces in which the identification of sequential points of time must be identified. The interior design of the house has evolved from a collaboration between the architect and his client, who is an engineer. The progression through the house – vertically, diagonally, horizontally and laterally – is a fantastic sequence of events with expanding and contracting vistas. This experience is made very dynamic when the children of the house are running up and down the stairs, and the whole structure can be perceived as a children's playground.

2nd floor

view from south-west >

PORNCHAI BOONSOM

The formal architectural qualities of the house, though borrowing much from the Deconstruction movement, can be seen as a response to the surrounding chaos of Bangkok. It is possible to think that such wilfully non-traditional architecture is appropriate for the confusion and complexity of the city.

PIRAK ANURAKYAWACHON

1st floor bedroom

entry from south

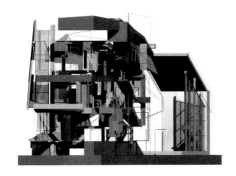

section

section

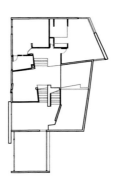

2nd floor plan

1st floor plan

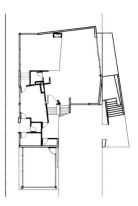

ground floor plan

MnG House Bangkok, Thailand 2001

view from 1st floor

PETER SKINNER AND
ELIZABETH WATSON-BROWN

St Lucia House St Lucia, Brisbane, Qld, Australia 1999

Two architects who had practised separately - he in academia, she in private practice - collaborated for the first time in twenty years, on the design of their own home in St Lucia, a Brisbane suburb densely packed with small single house sites and apartments lining the Brisbane River. The result is a deliberate experiment in alternative suburban living in the sub-tropics. The guiding idea of Peter Skinner and Elizabeth Watson-Brown's house is effectively a giant double-height glazed verandah or a completely transparent *piano nobile*. But instead of timber lattice, roll-down blinds, or an exaggerated roof overhang to shade the house, the architects used the presence of three very large, fully grown and sculpturally spectacular trees to act as their climatic foil. At night, the house reads as a three-dimensional illuminated Japanese screen, and the life of the house is discreetly veiled from the street by the tree's artful limbs. However what is also described at night is the way in which this house works.

It is as if a multi-level courtyard house, or a spatially complex Corbusian villa, has been peeled back to reveal itself. The rear wall of the central double-height kitchen/dining/living space is in fact the back wall of the house. The master bedroom is elevated above this

north elevation

living area from east >

major space, and the balustrade of its outdoor deck penetrates the main space, emphasising the gesture of the large signature volume. The grand spatial gesture is in fact subtly controlled, and it is rich rather than simplistic. The house is effectively zoned into five interlocking levels, and the front courtyard becomes a multi-level outdoor stage set for domestic life within a compact suburban site. The monumental central living room exaggerates the scale of the small house and its garden, and proposes that living in the sub-tropics need not be solely concerned with breezes and a rain-shedding roof - that space itself might act as its own natural exhaust device, and that the prospect and shelter of a tree might transform one's mind as well as provide necessary shade.

PHILIP GOAD

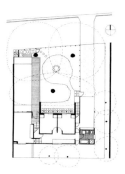

ground floor plan

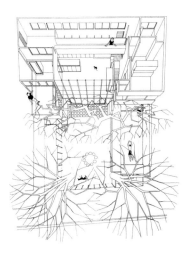

aerial perspective

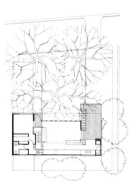

1st floor plan

living area from west

WOHA ARCHITECTS

Hua Guan House Singapore 1999–2001

rear circulation gallery

< view from north-east

Wong Mun Summ and Richard Hassell have practised together in Singapore as WOHA since 1994, and have gained a reputation for their design versatility: elegant, project specific architecture is their strength. The architects are interested in form as an abstract language with which to design, organize and express the concepts of a project. Organization is key, as WOHA always looks for a strong concept with relatively few but repetitive components which, when refined and developed, will produce a unique project.

In the case of the Hua Guan House, the architects wanted a house that was a simple idea, "a row of rooms along a pool, which had the quality of a verandah". Unlike most projects in Singapore, the clients, the Tan family, welcomed the tropical "sunlight streaming in but the tropical heat kept out; large windows kept open even during thunderstorms" experiences related to verandah life.

The house was pushed back against the property line, following a semi-detached mode, to maximize open space and orient all views towards the garden, with its 25 metre lap pool flanked by a pool deck and a pool pavilion. The house itself is tucked underneath a large overhanging roof. The bedrooms each have a pod that cantilevers out over the pool, allowing each room to engage with the outdoor entertaining areas. The bedrooms are screened by sliding and folding timber screens, which when opened fully, transform the pods into balconies. A circulation gallery separates the linear body of the house from the party wall. The gallery is formed from the party wall wrapping up and over, and is top-lit from a clerestory window, providing soft, indirect light down the wall to the koi pond and reflection pool below. A glass bridge allows the koi carp to be enjoyed from above like a living Chinese painting.

The Tan family collect contemporary Chinese scroll paintings, and appreciate paintings that have bold strokes and striking compositions. In this project the architects use layering to create a sense of depth in the same manner that Chinese paintings layer back to create pictorial depth. The wrapping, folding language was continued throughout the project, from the black boundary walls and timber elements to the custom designed cabinets and loose furniture.

For WOHA, a density of experience, and a "lushness" in environment are the desired outcomes in residential design, and many design decisions are about intensifying experiences through orchestration and layering.

ANOMA PIERIS

living area

living area to pool

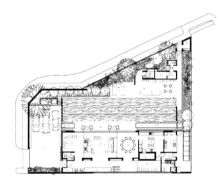
ground floor plan

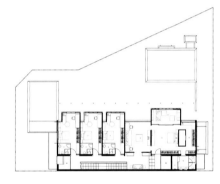
1st floor plan

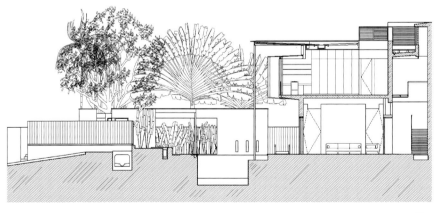
section

Hua Guan House Singapore 1999–2001

view from north-west

ADI PURNOMO

Ciganjur House Jakarta, Indonesia 2003

kitchen and north-west courtyard

< view from south-west

Renovating a 350m² home unit situated on a 1000m² site in southern Jakarta, Adi Purnomo and his client proposed a rethink of the common perceptions of inhabitation. Going through an intensive design process, the rigid program of the existing house was transformed into a fluid spatial network. Reprogramming was instigated by the family's wish to have an open house where boundaries between exterior and interior are softened, and where activities unfold as a continuous process. This vision is met by the architect's contention that a house provides ongoing cultivation of family life, demanding 'smooth' spatial arrangements. Purnomo also offers a critique of the way conventional urban house designs create a totally internalised lifestyle, wherein exterior living is abandoned due to unpleasant weather and to security concerns. These problems often detach urban dwellers from their natural and social environment.

This renovation of two one-storey buildings features the amalgamation of room units into two zones of activities, private and public, and the mediation between interior and exterior spaces.

Private zones of bedroom and bathroom units are carefully arranged and positioned around a public area of

ADI PURNOMO

living, dining and kitchen. This secures privacy while minimizing disengagement between the private and public zones. The arrangement defines the enclosure and flow of the open plan public zone, while consciously working to optimize the existing layout and to minimize the new wall length. Transitional spaces open the house into the landscape. These areas, in the form of open terraces, an open carport, and small ponds, are instrumental in physically and visually stretching the interior space, in accommodating the extension of interior activities, and in maximising the inclusion of the exterior within the interior spatial experience. The link between the main house and the secondary wing, containing service and creative activities, is established by means of landscaping, open corridors and house openings. The two houses are arranged as one integrated system.

The terraces feature loose corals and wooden surfaces lain over porous organic fibres mixed with corals, allowing surface water penetration into the ground. The sound of the loose corals underfoot is a poetic reminder of nature. A careful selection of low cost building materials and finishes minimized both cost and the use of chemical substances.

The renovation maintains the existing house size while fundamentally improving the quality of the spatial experience and cultivation of family life.

AMANDA ACHMADI

view from west

entry from east

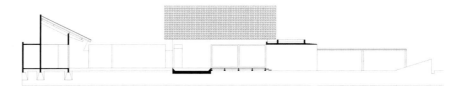

section

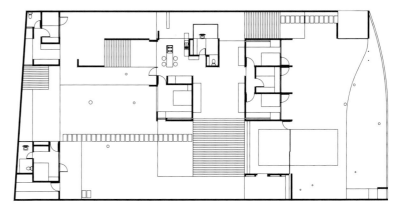

floor plan

Ciganjur House Jakarta, Indonesia 2003

view from east

KERSTIN THOMPSON

House at Lake Connewarre Leopold, Vic, Australia 2002

The House at Lake Connewarre first appears as a black smudge in the landscape, a continuation of the dark shadows of the pine trees surrounding the northern end of the site, which was old degraded farmland on the edge of a tidal lake. Approaching by car along the sweeping driveway, the house reveals itself, flattening out for its full epic length. The house traces the ridge of a steep escarpment, amplifying its dramatic edge and buckling with the shape of the land.

The positioning of the house divides the large site into two: a northern front yard with a new landscape which grades from the exotic at the boundary to the indigenous, and a southern back yard with indigenous planting running down to the lake. The building is designed as an integral component of the landscape, a windbreak on the ridge, an interval on the horizon.

In discussing the house size, Kerstin Thompson describes it in terms of a 'house-as-resort'. Part of the challenge was how to design a big building without ostentation, and the architects pointedly made use of conventional construction and do not pursue craft for its own sake. There is a matter-of-factness in the finishes and materials, allowing the house to be described by

elevated view from north

view from north >

KERSTIN THOMPSON

Thompson as a 'weatherboard shack.' Its 'ordinariness' enabled the budget to be directed toward achieving the required floor-space area.

The house has three pavilions: a guest house/recording studio, a garage and store, and the main house – all linked by a folded roof. Numerous spaces are created between the pavilions, as places of shelter and framing views. To the north, a timber-clad enclosed pool deck is inserted into the landscaped front yard, with a full height glass wall linking it to the main house. Circulation within the house is, in part, along this north glass wall, and is designed as a significant part of the experience of the interior, with space opening and narrowing, and views captured and lost, as the internal geometry of the walls shifts. The ply floor panels maintain a normalising geometry throughout, and a long strip window to the south frames spectacular views over the lake, stretching the length of the vast cranked wall containing the major rooms. The dining room opens to the southwest with a high glazed corner, marking it as a room of great occasion.

This is a clever and sophisticated house, consciously referencing the suburban and stretching its scale into something streamlined, strong and remarkably elegant.

GEOFFREY LONDON

south elevation

interior looking east

site plan

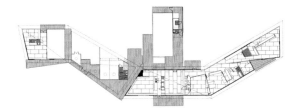

floor plan

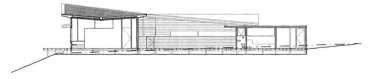

section

House at Lake Connewarre Leopold, Vic, Australia 2002

south deck looking east

living area

SEKSAN DESIGN

Sekeping Serendah House Serendah, Malaysia 2000

The astonishing recent urban sprawl of Kuala Lumpur has occurred to the south and west, as the city is hemmed in to the north by the slopes of Malaysia's main range of mountains, where limestone peaks rise dramatically from the rainforest. Here, the narrow roads are lined with kampungs, and the *orang asli* (indigenous people) live throughout the region. Two prototype 'tents' made from glass, steel and timber sit on a sloping site surrounded by an *orang asli* forest reserve. A bubbling brook, coloured red from iron oxide washed down the mountains, flows through the site.

These 'glorified tents' consist of 2 stacked square rooms, with entry from below through a hatch in the steel-grate and timber deck. An open-air bathroom space is at the rear. The steel-frame construction elements were reduced as far as possible in size and quantity to have the houses sitting lightly on the site. Extensive glazing maximises the view while minimising the impact of the structures on the forest. Custom-orb zincalume was used for the roof and other cladding. "I love the idea and look of the sheds in shanty towns", notes Ng Sek San "and it reflects my political affiliations most accurately."

1st floor

ground floor

south elevation and deck >

SEKSAN DESIGN

Sek San is a structural engineer, landscape designer, architectural innovator and eco-soldier. He proudly claims that no tree was felled during the construction of the Serendah prototypes, which were designed and built in collaboration with Carolyn Lau and Tam Mei Sim. Acknowledging that the formal qualities of the houses were inspired by Peter Stutchbury's seminal Israel House (1992) north of Sydney, Sek San suggests that the appropriate use of materials, and the honest yet decorative detailing, exemplified by Peter Stutchbury and other Australian architects could be widely applied in tropical Asia.

PATRICK BINGHAM-HALL

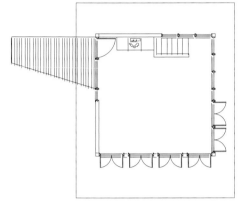

1st floor plan

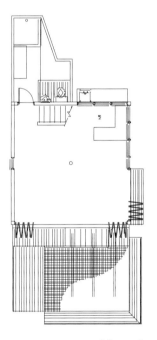

ground floor plan

section

view from south-east

CY KUAN

Courtyard House Bali, Indonesia 2003

view from east

< entry to house

A traditional form of dwelling in Bali is the house compound, a walled enclosure containing a number of *bale* (hipped roof pavilions) for eating, sleeping and working. It is a model that has been reinterpreted endlessly by resort architects to provide detached villa accommodation for hotel guests. In this private house set on the edge of a jungle landscape, CY Kuan has subverted that common interpretation. He has instead created a serene courtyard dwelling – with no freestanding pavilions – but with open covered spaces connected to the enclosing perimeter courtyard walls. The house is thus not located within a courtyard but forms it. At the same time, the traditional notion of entry through blank walls is maintained, as is the idea of the screen wall (*aling-aling*) to obstruct the entry of evil spirits.

Arrival at the house occurs through a series of wall openings, flanked by pools planted with lilies and sculptural grasses. The simplicity of the architecture is offset by the greater role played by the cultivated landscape between these walls: a frangipani tree framed against water and stone, and a broad reflecting pool that emphasises the picturesque outline of the trees above. The house, a discreet diagram of horizontals and verticals, is politely subservient to the landscape.

The other inversion, that suggests an architecture reaching beyond conventional conceptions in recent Balinese architecture, is the choice of materials. This house is about concrete, stone and water. It's not a lightweight timber pavilion but a gracious series of walls, sequential paths, and carefully framed axial vistas. This is not a primitive hut but an urbane villa, reaching its climax in an open terrace overlooking the dramatic view. Behind is the open lawn of the garden; ahead is the sublime silhouette of the jungle. This is the contemplative hinge-point of the house, between the nurtured landscape of the courtyard and the wilderness beyond.

PHILIP GOAD

living room and courtyard

pool and courtyard

west pavilion

courtyard from east

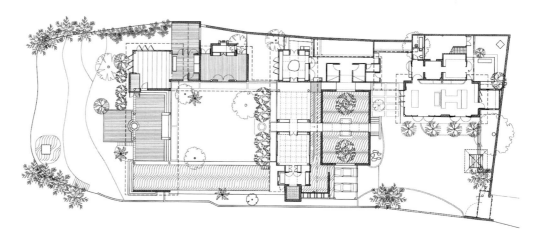
site plan

Courtyard House Bali, Indonesia 2003

view from south-west

INDEX

HOUSES FOR THE 21ST CENTURY

Rawhiti House Northland, New Zealand 1999
Architect: Fearon Hay